ELAINE WALSTER

G. WILLIAM WALSTER

a new look at Love

ADDISON-WESLEY
PUBLISHING COMPANY

Reading, Massachusetts
Menlo Park, California
London • Amsterdam
Don Mills, Ontario • Sydney

Illustrations on pages 14, 27, 30, 32, 35, 44, 69, 81,
88, 105, 122, 125, 133, 147, 150, 170, 172
by Darcy Abrahams.

Library of Congress Cataloging in Publication Data

Walster, Elaine Hatfield, 1937-
  A new look at love.

  Bibliography: p.
  Includes index.
  1. Love. 2. Mate selection. 3. Inter-
personal relations. 4. Sex (Psychology)
I. Walster, G. William, 1941-   joint author.
II. Title.
HQ734.W195   301.41   77-92091
ISBN 0-201-08350-7
ISBN 0-201-08351-5 pbk.

Library of Congress Catalog Card No. 77-92091.

ISBN 0–201–08350–7 H
ISBN 0–201–08351–5 P
ABCDEFGHIJ–DO–798

Dedicated to my sisters
Mary Hatfield
and
Patricia Hatfield Rich
EW

Introduction

by T. George Harris

On love, everybody's an expert. Most of us figure, as Mark Twain would say, that on the basics of romance, if not the fancier frills, we know as much as the next person and maybe a damn sight more. Out of common knowledge and personal experience, for instance, just about anyone knows that:

• Women, being more concerned with such matters, generally fall in love before men do and then keep on carrying the torch after the men have called it quits.

• To be popular with the opposite sex, the three biggest factors are good looks, personality, and money.

• Familiar people—the woman or guy next door—usually lose out to the fascinating strangers we meet away from our normal life and work.

• In spite of brief infatuations and all the clichés about love at first sight, the passionate and breathless stage does not reach its peak until a romance has been building up for six to thirty months, maybe longer.

• For all their talk about warm-blooded women, men are generally turned off when they find a woman who's easy to get.

• Being more physical than women, men lose more sleep when in love, feel more spine tingles and other physical sensations, and experience a stronger sense of general well-being.

• As suggested by the dumb-blonde notion, physically attractive men and women tend to be looked on by others as colder, dumber, and less moral than the plainer people.

Ho hum, you say. So what's new? What's new is that the seven clichés you just read are all lies. They are the direct opposites of recent findings in psychological research. Now, for the first time, we have research on our intimate bonds—not just the usual opinions, often contradictory, that all sound equally true. We now know that many of the things we believe are *not* so, while others stand the rigorous test of scientific experiment. A small band of first-rate psychologists in several major universities have, over the last eight years, built the first solid body of research on love. Their work has roused bitter debate, as we shall see, and set them up for attacks not unlike those upon Kinsey's first studies of sex. But some have kept at it. In this book, the leading researcher gives the first overview of their findings.

We now have well-designed experiments, for instance, to wipe out the common notion that women fall in love first and carry the torch longer. At the University of Michigan, researchers have studied a large sample of dating couples over a long period of time. In a solid majority of the cases, the men fell in love first, while the women remained skeptical or uninterested. And it was usually the woman who called it all off, while the man marched on with torch in hand.

Then there's the ancient question of the easy-to-get woman. Generations of mothers and morals mongers have preached to young women that men will not respect or appreciate the girl who falls. Thousands of romantic novels, old and new-old, have been based on this notion. More recently, the dogma on campus has been turned around: the hard-to-get woman is not only frigid, perhaps out of touch with her deeper self, but not much of a real person. The new dogma, while less harsh, is no less unreal.

Elaine Walster set out several years ago to test the "easy-to-get" theory. Herself a beautiful and sensitive woman, she knew from her students how urgent the question continues to be. She first tested the older theory that the hard-to-get woman earns male respect and appreciation. The forbidden apple. But the experiment failed; no significant findings. So she tested to see if easy-to-get women were the winners. No luck. She finally came upon the obvious answer and checked it out. The finding was so obvious that she wondered why she, or thousands of others, had ever been caught by the prevailing clichés: Men want women who are easy for *them* to get, difficult for others.

Dr. Walster and her co-researchers have run dozens of studies on physical beauty. Intrigued by the dumb-blonde cliché, they did experiments with beautiful people, male and female, to see how others judged them and how beauty influenced their lives. Here, again, she shocked a lot of hypocrites. In spite of all the self-righteous talk about plain people being the good, most of us unconsciously assume that beautiful people are the best people. We see the physically attractive man or woman as brighter, nicer, warmer, and more successful in all things.

Our prejudice against the ugly duckling, Walster found, is well developed by the time we are in grade school. Teachers and pupils alike expect the worst from the unattractive ones—and their expectations often become self-fulfilling prophecies. And, in spite of our ethnic variety, Americans tend toward a stereotyped notion of physical beauty. We tend to agree on who is the beautiful woman, who is the handsome man. They both go through life, and courtships, collecting a lot of free points.

So do people with money and attractive personalities. But here, again, Walster comes through with a surprise. Good looks, money, and personality all influence the romance market, but none of them ranks as the most important determinant of who will be popular, who will have the most active social life or, for that matter, the best sex life. What counts more than anything else is being relaxed. By the kind of statistical analysis that physicists use to determine the character of tiny particles, social psychologists have found that it's the easy-going, relaxed man or woman who most attracts the opposite sex.

You may remember reading about Elaine and William Walster in the newspapers or in *People* magazine. They are the beautiful, hard-working pair of professors who were photographed in bed. They met when she was a graduate student teaching psychology at Stanford University and he was an undergraduate interested in statistics and computers. Soon married, the Walsters took appointments together as junior faculty at the University of Minnesota and then at the University of Rochester before moving in 1967 to the University of Wisconsin at Madison. Being a woman in the sexist groves of academe, Elaine had worked at marginal jobs and been denied tenure in situations where a man would have automatically been tenured. Wisconsin's sociology department gave her tenure first as an associate professor, then in 1968 as a full professor. Once she had this solid base, she moved ahead fast in the field of research that she cared about most: the ordinary, basic questions of love in everyday life. The editors of *Psychology Today,* then a group of brilliant young Ph.D.'s and magazine journalists, began to rely on her sound but fascinating discoveries. She is, in my judgment, the leading researcher in the new studies of love, but without Bill's steady backing she would have been unable to continue her first-rate work under the attacks she has endured.

The most damaging blow fell about three years ago. Wisconsin's own Senator Proxmire discovered that the National Science Foundation in Washington had given Elaine and one of her research partners—Dr. Ellen Berscheid of the University of Minnesota—an $84,000 grant to continue work on passionate and companionate love. The senator, while often a thoughtful watchdog of the public pocketbook, gleefully fired off an idiotic press release:

> I object to this not only because no one—not even the National Science Foundation—can argue that falling in love is a science; not only because I'm sure that even if they spend $84 million or $84 billion they wouldn't get an answer that anyone would believe. *I'm also against it because I don't want the answer.*
>
> I believe that 200 million other Americans want to leave some things in life a mystery, and right at the top of things we don't want to know is why a man falls in love with a woman and vice versa. . . .
>
> So National Science Foundation—get out of the love racket. Leave that to Elizabeth Barrett Browning and Irving Berlin. Here if anywhere Alexander Pope was right when he observed, "If ignorance is bliss, tis folly to be wise." [Italics added]

Proxmire's joke could have been worth a chuckle, but the fact is that he was deadly serious. NSF backed down from further support, though it insisted the senator's comments were not the reason. The Walster-Berscheid grant had been the only NSF funds being given to women social psychologists that year, but Proxmire had not bothered with such niceties. His attack was a cheap shot and it was tempting to respond in kind. After all, since the senator had recently patched a bald spot, he obviously agreed with Walster's findings about beautiful people. Instead, I wrote him an open letter about not having done his homework before taking a hip-shot, mailed him the letter, and then published it as a personal column in *Psychology Today* magazine. He never replied.

The general press had a field day with Proxmire's joke, as he expected. "We already know why people fall in love," declared a retired bishop in the *Detroit News,* though his excellence never enlightened us as to what it is we know. Other media took Walster's side, and Senator Barry Goldwater came to her defense. In *The New York Times,* James Reston wryly agreed that love will always be a mystery. "But if the sociologists and psychologists can get even a suggestion," Reston concluded, "of the answer to our pattern of romantic love, marriage, disillusions, divorce—and the children left behind—it would be the best investment of federal money since Jefferson made the Louisiana Purchase."

Reston's sentence hits the problem on the nose. Love has depths of mystery that no researcher will ever invade. We need not worry that the sweet uncertainties will be wiped out, for the ultimate experience available to any man or woman is the close encounter with the mind and body of another soul. Even mystical religious experiences, reports sociologist Andrew Greeley, are associated with sexual ecstasy; John Milton recognized this fact when he let Adam know God through knowing Eve. But the limits on what we can know about love, like the limits on our final knowledge about anything, do not drive us to Proxmire's know-nothing stance.

The underlying crisis of our time, it seems to me, has to do with those problems of trust and intimacy that we discover in passionate love, and in the aftermath, if we are lucky, that is—true companionship. The divorce rate is but one crude indicator of our culture's total confusion. All our guide-posts have been knocked down. For better or worse, today's young adults have no confidence in the rules nervously passed on to them by their parents. Indeed, this generation is sure of but one thing: their parents were wrong. The one source of authority they trust in this area, as we discovered at *Psychology Today,* comes with the patient work of careful researchers. To fail to provide the best work possible, it seems to me, is to deny water to parched mouths.

Elaine Walster, teaching courses on love at the University of Wisconsin, has for years listened to the urgent questions of her students. They are not worried about wiping out love's mystery. They are instead eager for any clues that might offer a deepened experience and let them take one step beyond the painful clichés.

In this book, truly *A New Look at Love,* the Walsters combine research and insight to get as close as they can to answers to the ordinary questions. At the risk of seeming unliberated, though she is a strong feminist, Elaine insists on facing up to the fact that women want men, as men want women. She does not hesitate to give practical advice on how to search, advice backed up by research. (To give you another hint of what's ahead, the hunt for a partner, like any other hunt, often comes down to traffic patterns. But before such a search can be hopeful, the woman has to get rid of her dream of finding the ideal male.)

Elaine has a kind of courage not often seen in researchers, or anywhere else for that matter, and, in psychology, courage is a prerequisite to originality. Journalists and other outsiders rail against psychology's addiction to rat experiments, but this criticism misses the deeper failure. The faithful rat, as one of our mammalian cousins, has helped us learn a great deal, and a bold researcher can ask the rat very useful questions through an experiment. Experimental psychology becomes a bore in many universities simply because it does not ask worthwhile questions. It takes guts to break out and ask new questions, especially a question worth asking. It takes a hell of a lot of guts to ask, as Elaine does, questions about love and caring. Like Senator Proxmire, senior faculty members delight in putting down such questions with a joke.

One reason for their caution comes from a little-understood distinction among people who call themselves psychologists. You have probably read plenty of books and articles about love written by "psychologists." Until now, these books have been by clinical psychologists, often Freudians, who do little or no research. Such books may report on fascinating case studies, say of a man with an Oedipus complex who keeps falling in love with women who look like his mother. Others use the latest popular psychological theory to explain every problem and preach upbeat solutions. Lacking real research, such material just adds another opinion to our increasing confusion about what goes on between men and women. Research psychologists have often been afraid to go into this field precisely because other psychologists have so muddied the waters.

Walster and the researchers on whom she reports in this book belong to a very different breed. I like to think of them as the accountants of everyday life. Instead of jumping to conclusions, they ask questions—at their best, very mundane and basic questions—and then design studies to give them facts about behavior that answer the question. That's why we are, for the first time, beginning to be able to sort out the lies about love from the facts.

Poets and philosophers and psychoanalysts have given us thousands of contradictory answers to the problems of love. In this sense, there is nothing new to be said. But if you can pick a pair of contradictory clichés and find which one comes closer to the truth, we can then move on to a more useful question. Otherwise, our thoughts keep circling around the same inanity, like the old one about the easy-to-get woman.

Pushing on beyond such hang-ups, the Walsters have been putting the research together, theirs and others, into a more general framework that permits us to think more sensibly about love. They have proposed "equity theory," a body of thought that tends to shock many other researchers and readers. Especially after passionate love cools into a longer-lasting relationship—companionate love—couples tend to strike a balance in terms of what they contribute to the coupling. Beauty and money may be the trade-off against brains and warm giving. Whatever the bargain, the Walsters believe that we negotiate in intimate relations as we do in life's other transactions.

You can imagine the rage that idea rouses. Romantics insists that love conquers all; they consider the idea of trade-offs a blasphemy against the very notion of consuming love. Marxists in several universities attack equity theory on predictable grounds: Sure, they say, that's just another twisting of our souls by the commercial corruption of capitalism. Under true Marxist "consciousness," they believe, love would be unconditional— no hidden bargains in the bedroom. Love researchers are now in all-out war around the Walster theory.

You will see in the later chapters how strong a case the Walsters make. For instance, inequitable relationships tend to fall apart. Even those who get more than they give, like those who give more than they get, tend to feel acute discomfort. And the one who gives more than he or she gets tends to be the one who has an extramarital affair.

But you'll soon be reading the facts from the Walsters themselves. You will, I hope, enjoy the book as much as I've enjoyed watching the Walsters do the research and go through three drafts of the chapters. However, so as not to leave you hanging, maybe I ought to report the facts that have replaced the seven lies I made up at the beginning of this introduction. Please forgive my trickery, but I don't know any other way to get across the difference between opinion and research facts about the ties that bind us together:

• Women tend to be LIFO, last-in-first-out of romance, while men are FILO, first-in-last-out. If you happen to know how these two terms are used in business accounting, you'll have fun remembering this plain little fact about everyday courtship.

• There's a practical point to pick up from the fact that it's the relaxed men and women who win the popularity sweepstakes. The woman who primps hard before a date, and thus tenses herself up for the encounter, makes herself overly anxious and becomes less than her genial best.

• Most men marry the girl next door, or at the next desk, or at least somebody they find in a familiar environment. Look around. . . .

• Melancholy as it seems, the passionate, breathless stage lasts only six to thirty months. Elaine interprets the data to say that it's longer than Bill believes it to be, but either way we can't hope to live high on a romantic cloud. But both Walsters say companionate love can, over the years, climb back to brief days of spine-tingling. . . .

• The easy-to-get woman, or man: You know the facts, and I'm not about to suggest a practical application.

• Women's bodies are kinder to them, more generous, because in passionate love they feel more physical highs, though they also lose more sleep.

• Now that we know our hidden prejudice against plain people, we can free ourselves of that bigotry.

"I love the idea of there being two sexes, don't you?"

Preface

In the last few years, we've taught a course on human sexuality to thousands of students at the University of Wisconsin. After class, students inevitably drop by to chat. They ask an amazing array of questions:

- How can I tell if he loves me—or if he's just handing me a line?
- Why do I always fall in love with the wrong people?
- What is realistic to expect from a relationship?
- Women always say they love me "like a brother." What's wrong?
- Do open marriages work?

In addition we've gotten hundreds of letters from people with romantic and marital problems. A distraught Army colonel asked: "Does love always sort of drift away? Is there any way that love can survive repeated absences? I used to take the Greyhound from San Francisco to Portland just to talk to her for a few minutes. Now we don't seem to care if we're together or not. Is such apathy normal? Do all marriages just sort of fizzle out?"

An eighteen-year-old secretary telephoned us and said she was desperately in love with a man: "Every time I see him my heart beats fast and drops to my stomach; whenever he's near I love to have him touch me. He is all I've ever wanted. The problem? He may have some mafia connections. I really don't want to think about it. Should I risk marrying him?"

We've heard many of these concerns and questions again and again. The aim of this book is to provide *some* of the answers. For the past fifteen years, we have been studying why and how people are attracted to each other and fall in love. This is a new area of social-psychological research and scientists are only beginning to understand the complexities of love.

Social psychologists pride themselves on formulating clear theories, testing their hypotheses in scientific ways, and—even then—being a little skeptical about their results. Only with great trepidation would social psychologists ever generalize their findings to the real world. They always keep in mind that although social-psychological principles may be true for most people, they never apply to everyone; there are exceptions to all rules.

The problem with such a cautious approach is that it makes it very difficult for scientists to communicate with men and women caught up in real-life problems. What we all want is the scientists' *best guess* as to what actions are likely to be rewarding and which are not. We don't want to slog through scientists' cautions on the limitations of their research. Most of us take that for granted. What we want are suggestions.

In this book, we try to tell you what social psychologists know about love relationships *so far*. The information here should begin to shed new light on the age-old mysteries of love. Our intention was to write a readable, useful, and accurate book that could help you answer some of your own questions about love. We hope we have succeeded.

Madison, Wisconsin   EW
March 1978   GWW

Acknowledgments

This book started out with the title *Passionate Love.* The original manuscript was a rather lumbering encyclopedia of existing research. A number of our friends—Dorothy Loeb, Jane Traupmann, Mary Utne, Miguel Reyes, and Julia Hay; Philip Wexler, Ellen Berscheid, Eve and Vaughan Loudenback, T. George Harris, Ann Dilworth, and Cathy Redlich—painstakingly read and reread successive drafts of the manuscript, which eventually evolved into *A New Look at Love.* We'd like to thank them formally for their helpful critiques. We'd also like to thank Darcy Abrahams for contributing her impossible illustrations. We appreciate Elinor Loucks' and Jean Padrutt's good nature in typing and securing permissions for this manuscript.

Contents

7

Companionate love:
you can't ~~always~~ *ever* get what you want   127

8

Passionate and companionate love:
making choices   159

one
What is this thing called love?

*Love is such a tissue of paradoxes,
and exists in such an endless variety
of forms and shades that you may say almost anything about it
that you please, and it is likely to be correct.*

Henry Finck
*Romantic Love and
Personal Beauty* (1902)

*Love is the strange bewilderment which overtakes one person
on account of another person.*

James Thurber and E. B. White
Is Sex Necessary?

What is love? That's a question we've all struggled with at one time or another. And usually, instead of arriving at a simple answer, we seem to come up with more questions: Can we love someone we hate? How is love different from infatuation? If we really want to know how people feel about us, should we pay attention to what they say, or to what they do? Is it true that we always hurt the one we love?

Although we all care keenly about our love affairs and devote an enormous amount of time to analyzing and worrying about them, most of us are baffled by such questions. This isn't really surprising. When our relationships are going well and we're swept up in the joy of getting to know someone, it doesn't occur to us to sit around wondering, "What went right?" And, when we're in the throes of a disastrous relationship, we're in no condition to calmly calculate what went wrong.

In this book, we hope to provide some answers to the questions about love that concern us all. Until recently, love was regarded simply as a mystery—provocative, exciting, and sometimes painful—and that was that. However, since the 1950s, scientists have started to research various aspects of this most elusive emotion. Some of their findings confirm commonsense notions about love that have passed from generation to generation. Other findings are quite startling. Taken all together, this information begins to shed some light on what love is, who finds it and who doesn't, and what causes love to flourish . . . or die.

PASSIONATE LOVE
AND COMPANIONATE LOVE

Love can appear in two very different forms: passionate love and companionate love. Passionate love is a wildly emotional state, a confusion of feelings: tenderness and sexuality, elation and pain, anxiety and relief, altruism and jealousy. Companionate love, on the other hand, is a lower-key emotion. It's friendly affection and deep attachment to someone. Almost all of us make a sharp distinction between our passionate feelings and our companionate ones. Which is "true love"? People disagree sharply on this question.

We asked a number of people to describe to us what passionate love feels like for them. Here's what they said:

When I'm in love, I think about the man I'm in love with constantly, I can twist any conversation around in my mind to lead to him. When I see him—POW!—my heart takes a leap, my cheeks flush, and I can't help smiling. At night before going to bed, I think of all the little things we said or did throughout the day—and smile.

When I'm in love, I never look at any other guys with interest. If I know I'm not going to see him that day, I don't take pains to look nice.

Also, I always seem to be in a good mood. Of course, I do have a heart attack when he said he'd call at 6:30 and it's 6:35 and I haven't gotten a call yet—but . . . on the whole . . . it's terrific.

Bloomingdale's saleswoman, New York

I kept telling myself how much I hated Jed, how queer I thought he was. When he would talk to me, when I was with a group of people, I'd criticize him, ignore him, or sometimes just walk away. I was a classic bitch to him. Yet, somehow—unconsciously maybe—I seemed to find out everything about him. And I mean *everything*. But I still treated him like my worst enemy. Until one day he came up to me while I was alone and simply asked me, "Why do you hate me?" I replied, "Because I love you."

After that things went smoothly.

College woman, Wisconsin

Love is a feeling of belonging, having someone to identify with. To feel overwhelming trust and jealousy at the same time. *Everything* you do and think about is shared with the other. When you touch one another, or just hear their voice, there is a desperate feeling of want and need, a feeling inside that actually hurts. When I first felt love it was the best feeling in the world.

Dry cleaner's assistant, Nebraska

What does it feel like to be in love? The best kind of love is the chemistry you feel when there's someone watching you from across the room. You both know you're attracted; your chest is tight; your stomach is filled with butterflies. Other people talk to you, but you are oblivious. Your voice shakes and rises an octave. You become flustered when he talks to you . . . and the next day you remember, word for word, the conversation.

Nurse, Kansas

And here is what several others said about companionate love:

Being a romantic at heart I had very definite ideas about how "love" should be. Somehow, however, it didn't turn out the way I had imagined.

The earth didn't move, as I imagined it would. I feel comfortable with this man. I can communicate with him on all levels. He understands me.

Ex-nun, New Jersey

When I am with her, I feel secure. I think the thing that attracted me most, first of all, was her looks. Then after we had been going together awhile, I guess her stability became very important. Because I'm a free spirit, and she settled me down. It is like being a little kid again. It feels like you're with your mother; she keeps watching out for you. Saying don't get drunk, don't fight about this and that. When I need someone, she is always there.

An 18-year-old college student commenting
on his affair with a 25-year-old divorcée

Love means wanting the best for another. Love is often expressed by letting the other person know you believe in him/her and that you support them in what they are doing. You help them to grow as a person. You allow yourself to need the other. You support them to the extent of letting them know that you share the same fears and goals and dreams and hopes. You are willing to be vulnerable.

A Ford assembly-line worker, Detroit

A few people who wrote to us traced the evolution of their feelings from passionate to companionate love:

When I fell in love I felt fantastic! I glowed, people said they never saw me look prettier or happier. I felt this way, I think, because of the new self-confidence Ted gave me, and because of the feeling of just being needed and desired. This made my life exciting and worth living.

As it turned out, I married Ted. We're still very happy and very much in love, but there is a definite difference between the first passionate feelings of love and the now mellowed-out feelings.

Don't get me wrong, though, there are still plenty of passionate times. It's just that when you live together, the passion is not as urgent a thing. You're more loving friends.

Newlywed, Wisconsin

ORIGINS OF PASSIONATE LOVE

For centuries people have been trying to figure out what love is. Plato, Shakespeare, Napoleon, George Washington, Norman Mailer, Margaret Trudeau, and Charlie Brown all have attempted to describe this complex emotion. Theories about the origins of love abound. Let's look at some of the more interesting ones.

PLATO'S THEORY: THE LONGING FOR COMPLETION

The Greeks were among the first to try to define love. In the fifth century B.C., the philosopher Plato offered an intriguing theory about the origins of love in his *Symposium.* Originally, he contended, humanity was divided into three kinds of people: men, women, and the androgenous—a union of the two. Androgenous beings were round; their backs and sides formed a circle. They had one head with two faces (always looking in opposite ways), four ears, four hands, four feet, and two "privy" members. These beings could walk upright—either backwards or forwards, as they pleased. Or they could roll over at a great pace, turning nimbly on their four hands and four feet like tumblers.

Eventually, the gods and humanity came into conflict. Determined to cripple humanity forever, the gods cut the men, women, and androgenous beings into two parts, "like a Sorb-apple which is halved for pickling." Since the division, the cleft parts have wandered the earth, each searching for its lost half. In the Platonic scheme, the halves of the once-complete men became "the best of the lot." These individuals are valiant and manly; they embrace that which is like themselves (other men). The once-complete women do not care for men; they prefer lesbian attachments. The androgenous halves continue to seek *their* cleft portion: the male halves are lovers of women; the females are adulterous women who lust after men.

Thus, humanity is always longing for completion—longing to meld with another person. This, then, is the nature of love according to Plato.

THE FREUDIANS: FROM NARCISSISM TO ATTACHMENT

It is ironic that Sigmund Freud, who had so many insights on so many other things, had so little to say about love. Early in his career, Freud commented, "Up to the present, I have not found the courage to make any broad statements on the essence of love, and I think that our knowledge is not sufficient to do so." [1] He never found the courage to do so. At the end of his life, he confessed, "We really know very little about love."

Freud took the position—along with all the philosophers from Plato to Schopenhauer and all the psychologists from Spencer to Havelock Ellis —that love is sexual in its origin. Initially, infants are totally narcissistic— all their love is directed at themselves. Later, through a tangled series of transformations and countertransformations, children begin to direct their love toward one of their parents. These feelings are intensely powerful. Finally, adults reluctantly transfer their love to an ultimately appropriate object—a member of the opposite sex. In the normal man or woman, this love consists of a combination of two currents of feelings—tender affection and sensuality.

Freud observed that love must always prove a little disappointing because of the incest barrier:

> ... The ultimate object selected is never the original one but only a surrogate for it. Psychoanalysis has shown us, however, that when the original object of an instinctual desire becomes lost in consequence of repression, it is often replaced by an endless series of substitute objects, none of which ever give full satisfaction.[2]

Actually, it was a Neo-Freudian, Theodor Reik, who had the most to say about love. Reik contended that love and sex are profoundly different in origin and nature:

> What is the aim of sex? ... the disappearance of a *physical* tension, a discharge and a *release*. What is the aim of the desire we call love? The disappearance of a *psychical* tension, *relief*. ... Sex wants satisfaction; love wants happiness. Sex can be casual about its object. Love cannot. Love is always a personal relationship. The sex urge hunts for lustful pleasure; love is in search of joy and happiness.[3]

Like Freud, Reik says that infants are entirely narcissistic at first. However, unlike Freud, Reik believes that narcissistic love is, and will always remain, the unconscious reflection of others' admiration and appreciation.

Then comes the day when the world, which up to now has so lovingly provided for us, turns sour.

> The baby learns that his mother can be dissatisfied with him, that she can withdraw her affection if he does not behave as she wishes, that she can be angry or cross. ... The possibility of losing his mother's love certainly strikes the child with a force which can no more be coped with than an earthquake. ...[4]

The realization that we are not loved anymore is such a shock that only many repetitions can make us understand it. What can we do about it? An infant's first response is to become angry. He screams with rage. This doesn't work. He's forced to try a more devious strategy:

> The little boy thus demonstrates in his own behavior what he wants his mother to do to him, how she should behave to him. He announces this wish by displaying his tenderness and affection toward his mother who gave these before to him.[5]

This childish reaction is the prototype of later love:

Our display of loving is the anticipation of the love we desire from the other person. It is as if we were to demonstrate: I would like you to be thus wild about me. It is obvious that we act out a fantasy in this two-role play. We are both the other person whose love we yearn for and the beloved which we want to be. Our love is the unconscious advertisement of how we wish to be loved. It is a demonstration by proxy. We act toward the other person the way we would like the other to act toward us. In this way we unconsciously announce what we miss and what we long for.[6]

When we're in love, we are aware only of a powerful passion. Reik suggests, however, that there is more to love than meets the lover's eye. Hostility and envy lurk just below the surface, as much a part of love as affection and tenderness. Reik goes on to say that "he who asserts that love is altruistic is sadly mistaken. It is as selfish as breathing, but this self has changed, it has incorporated another being."[7] In profound love, it *is* as blessed to give as to receive. Such love is not unselfish love, of course. We give to ourselves when we give to the other.

Freud and Reik are helpful in explaining the origins of love. But what rekindles love later in life? According to Reik, all of us have impossibly elevated ego ideals. We long to be good-looking, young, strong, and clever. Now and then, we become uneasily aware of our shortcomings. We experience a vague dissatisfaction with ourselves and a lingering dislike. "These moods may run the gamut of dissatisfaction from twilight to darkness, from a wish to escape it all (often oneself too) to a real disgust of life."[8]

When people feel such self-disgust, three alternatives are open to them. First, they can moderate their demands on themselves. Obvious as this may seem, pride usually stands in the way. Not until we become very old are we able to accept being anything less than perfect.

So, instead, people choose one of two other paths. Sometimes they fall in love. They observe that someone near them seems to possess all the perfection they desire. At first, although they aren't consciously aware of this, the discovery makes them envious. Then, suddenly, the barrier between the two individuals melts, their tiresome egos vanish, and they begin to love. Now they long to be one with their beloved, to fuse with them, to merge into one being.

Of course, people who are dissatisfied with themselves might try to buttress their puny esteem in a quite different way. They may let hatred triumph by convincing themselves that they hate their ideal. In this case, it is love that remains below the surface. Thus, for Reik, love and hate have much in common. Love's opposite is not hatred—it is indifference.

THE SOCIAL PSYCHOLOGISTS: THE MIND AND THE BODY HAVE SOMETHING TO DO WITH IT

In 1964, Stanley Schachter, a psychologist at Columbia University, proposed a new theory of emotion. He argued that both our mind and body make a unique contribution to our emotional experiences; both must be in sync if we are to have a "true," spontaneous emotional experience.

Schachter's two-component theory helps us make sense of the passionate-love puzzle's jumble of pieces. For centuries, theorists have bitterly disagreed over what passionate love *really* is: Is it an intensely pleasurable experience or an intensely painful one? As soon as we adopt the Schachterian perspective, we have a ready answer: It's both.

It's all in your mind . . . or partly anyway

Our semiconscious assumptions about what we *should* be feeling in a given situation have a profound impact on what we *do* feel in that situation. By adolescence, our culture, our families, and our own experiences have instilled firm ideas in us as to what it is "appropriate" to feel at different times. We know that we should feel estatic when something unexpectedly good happens and depressed when everything goes awry. We are entitled to feel angry when we're humiliated and we ought to feel grateful when someone treats us more kindly than we deserve. Our assumptions about what we should feel determine what we do feel.

Society offers us many images of passionate love. As a consequence, we have the potential to experience passion in a wide variety of ways. Recently, when University of Minnesota psychologists asked college students, "What is passionate love?" they got strikingly different answers. Most students assumed that love is a very pleasurable state. They associated love with the joy of loving and being loved, with the pleasure of having someone *finally* understand you, with sexual fulfillment, with having fun, and so on. ("Oh, painful things *could* happen," they admitted, "but that's extremely rare.")

Some students' remarks, however, weren't so glowing. Love may have its moments, they said, but, all in all, it's a fairly unsettling state. They associated love with anxiety (would they be loved in return?), with emotional and sexual longing, and with uncertainty, confusion, and pain.

So, while love means pleasure for some, others equate it with pain. These very different ideas of passion profoundly affect our emotions and, ultimately, the ties we make in the name of love.

The body counts too

Schachter argues that all emotions have a second, indispensable component: intense physiological arousal. Joy, anger, passion, envy, and hate all are accompanied by telltale "symptoms"—a flushed face, a pounding heart, trembling hands, accelerated breathing.

Delightful experiences—like making love or simply talking with someone who loves and understands you—are physiologically arousing. Extremely painful experiences—like fear, jealousy, anger, rejection, or total confusion—are arousing too. Thus, either delight or pain (or a combination of the two) should have the potential for fueling a passionate experience.

Scientists have accumulated considerable support for the two-component theory. Both mind and body are critically important in shaping our emotions. Our minds determine what specific emotion we feel; our bodies determine whether or not we feel any emotion at all.

THE THREE THEORIES COMBINED

Is there any way we can combine the ideas of Plato, Freud, and the social psychologists—and a multitude of other theorists—to arrive at a more complete definition of passionate love? We think so. The following definition seems like a reasonable one:

> *Passionate love:* A state of intense absorption in another. Sometimes lovers are those who long for their partners and for complete fulfillment. Sometimes lovers are those who are ecstatic at finally having attained their partners' love and, momentarily, complete fulfillment. A state of intense physiological arousal.

THE ORIGINS OF COMPANIONATE LOVE

QUESTION

What is the difference between
liking and loving?

Liking and companionate love have quite a lot in common. Liking is simply the affection we feel for casual acquaintances. Companionate love is the affection we feel for those with whom our lives are deeply intertwined. The only real difference betwen liking and loving is the depth of our feelings and the degree of our involvement with the other person.

Couples are often interested in figuring out exactly how they feel about one another: "Do I really love my mate . . . or have we become just old friends?"

Given our definitions of liking and companionate love, it's easy to see why people find it so difficult to decide if they are "in love" or "in like." There is no real cutting point between the two; liking shades over imperceptibly into companionate love. Probably in any relationship, we drift in and out between the two.

Attraction theorists are generally agreed upon the genesis of liking and companionate love. In order to explain why we feel profoundly attracted to some people and why we can't stand others, theorists cite the principle of reinforcement: We like those who reward us and we dislike those who punish us. Psychologist Donn Byrne has fashioned from this commonsense observation a rather elegant reinforcement model of interpersonal attraction. Byrne's "Law of Attraction" looks like this:

$$Y = m \left[\frac{\Sigma \text{PR}}{(\Sigma \text{PR} + \Sigma \text{NR})} \right] + k$$

The Y in Byrne's formula stands for attraction. On the other side of the equation, the only symbols that really matter are PR (which stands for positive reinforcement—i.e., reward) and NR (which stands for negative reinforcement—i.e., punishment). Y (attraction) is greatest when there is a lot of PR and very little NR. In other words, you're likely to feel some fondness for the person who makes you feel marvelous about yourself and the world around you (the person who tells you you look pretty when you have a cold, who insists that you're smarter than your sister, who loans you his new suede jacket). And, you'll come to feel a distinct aversion toward someone who makes you feel rotten (someone who calls you a moron, makes you feel guilty about not calling home, leaves the dirty dishes in the sink three days in a row).

Your reaction to Byrne's "Law of Attraction" might be, "So what? Of course everybody longs for an intelligent, understanding, attractive, loving mate, someone who makes them feel secure yet allows them to be a free and independent person—they'd be crazy not to!" In other words, you might have figured out long ago that the best way to make someone love you is to make it very rewarding to be with you, and the best way to drive someone away is to fill that person's life with embarrassment, suffering, and pain. But you may not yet have made Byrne's further discovery that it doesn't end there. We also come to like people who are merely *associated* with good times and to dislike those who are merely *associated* with bad ones.

You've probably experienced this many times yourself. When you're spending a relaxed evening before the fire, drinking a fine wine, and listening to soft music, you often feel a rush of affection for anyone who happens to be around at the time. Conversely, when you haven't had a chance to

MISS PEACH

MISS PEACH by Mell Lazarus.
Courtesy of Mell Lazarus and
Field Newspaper Syndicate.

sit down all day, have a splitting headache, and the apartment is overflowing with dirty dishes and cat hair, you can't help but feel a little angry at the unfortunate person who unexpectedly drops by.

Psychologists have amassed considerable evidence for their contention that we all practice love—or guilt—by association. One psychologist tested the hypothesis that our reaction to people is colored by what we think of the environment they inhabit. He asked young people to get to know a stranger. Half of the men and women met in a cool, calm environment; the other half met in an uncomfortably hot room. The men and women who got to know each other in comfortable surroundings ended up liking each other a lot more than did the men and women who met under miserable conditions.[9]

Two other psychologists tested the same hypothesis by inviting men and women to look at and react to photographs of other men and women. Half of those judging the photographs met in a very pleasant room with beautiful draperies, soft lighting, elegant paintings and sculpture, and plush, comfortable chairs. The other half met in an ugly, shabbily furnished room with dirty, torn shades. The room was harshly lit by a bright, overhead bulb; the walls were stark and colorless; the tin ashtrays were full to overflowing; the room was neither swept nor dusted.

The authors predicted that when men and women met in the attractive room they'd feel relaxed and at ease—and would transfer their warm feelings to anything they were asked to judge. When they were in the ugly room, they'd feel depressed, repulsed, and disgusted and would transfer *those* feelings to anything they were asked to judge. The authors were right. Men and women who met in the beautiful room were far more receptive to the photographs than were men and women in the ugly room.[10]

So, one tip: If you and your lover want to establish a fledgling relationship—or keep the relationship you've got going strong—you should both be careful to do two things: (1) try to be rewarding partners in your own right, and (2) try to make sure that your times together continue to be good times. Maybe both of you *do* want to spend all your vacation time painting your apartment, repairing screens, and cleaning out your gutters and downspouts. Or maybe you do want to devote all of your energy to your job—working nights and weekends—and are willing to settle for a middling sex life, because you're "too tired" for anything else. Whatever your inclination, just remember: unless you're sharing some pretty good times *now,* you might not *have* a future together.

You've probably been exposed to half of this equation before. Guides to a happier marriage have always advised women to make sure their husbands associate them with pleasure—and not just with life's day-to-day irritations, drudgery, and frustration. They advise: "Meet him at the door beautifully dressed, with an ice cold martini in your hand." And the same marriage manuals warn husbands to see to it that their wives enjoy a satisfying sex life—or else. So far, so good.

But that's only half of the equation. What the manuals fail to say is that *you* must associate *your mate* with pleasure, too, if you're going to keep on loving. Romantic dinners, trips to the theater, evenings at home together, and vacations never stop being important. It's critical that you don't come to associate your partner with wet towels thoughtlessly dropped on the floor, barked-out orders, crying and nagging, or guilt ("You never say you love me"). If your relationship is to survive, it's important that you *both* continue to associate your relationship with good things. And this requires some effort and some thought.

THE TELLTALE SIGNS OF LOVE

QUESTION

How do I know when I'm in love?

ANSWER

When you think you are.

When we're physically aroused and when we label that unsettling feeling "love"—whether it's painful or enjoyable—then we're in love. It's that simple. Of course, people do a number of things which serve as a tip-off that they are in love.

Eye contact. When people are engaged in conversation, they gaze at one another for short periods. For example, a British scientist[11] found that in the normal course of events, people look at one another only 30–60 percent of the time. The more we like or love someone, the more we tend to sneak little glances at that person.[12]

One's "inclination" toward another. Sir Francis Galton, a Victorian psychologist, was the first to become intrigued by the realization that a person can assess another's character and personality without the other person realizing it. Galton conceived of an amazing array of schemes for invading privacy. Fortunately for his hapless victims, he never had time to carry out his elaborate ploys. He states:

> When two persons have an "inclination" to one another, they visibly incline or slope together when sitting side by side, as at a dinner table, and they then throw the stress of their weights on the near legs of their chairs. It does not require much ingenuity to arrange a pressure gauge with an index and dial to indicate changes in stress, but it is difficult to devise an arrangement that shall fulfill the three-fold condition of being effective, not attracting notice, and being applicable to ordinary furniture. I made some rude experiments, but being busy with other matters, have not carried them on, as I had hoped.[13]

More contemporary research supports Galton's notion that posture is a tip-off to our feelings—we tend to lean toward someone we like and away from someone we dislike.[14]

The distance one stands from another. People from different countries habitually stand different distances apart when conversing. Arab men generally stand very close to one another and feel comfortable walking together hand in hand. In Italy, it's not uncommon to see two men with their arms draped lovingly around one another. They like to be close enough to smell one another's scent and to feel one another's warmth. An American man, on the other hand, generally feels very uncomfortable if forced to stand extremely close to another man. In a crowded elevator or on a packed subway, American men stand rigid, careful not to touch.

The "correct" distance to stand apart is an unconscious social norm; people adjust to the proper distance automatically. The more we like someone, the closer we tend to stand. For example, Donn Byrne demonstrated that "standing distance" can serve as a useful index of romantic attraction. He introduced men and women students to each other and then sent the couples out on a thirty-minute "blind" coffee date. Eventually, the couples wandered back to the experimental office. As they checked in, the psychologist unobtrusively recorded how close to one another they were standing. Byrne found that the more the two students liked one another, the closer together they stood.[15]

Does the Byrne detection system work? Try it. Perhaps you know someone who is having an affair . . . and is trying desperately to keep

*The more we like someone, the closer we
tend to stand.*

people from finding out. Does he give himself away? At a cocktail party, does he stand closer to his wife . . . or to his mistress? Does he stand closer to his mistress or to the other women at the party?

KINESIS: THE SCIENCE OF BODY LANGUAGE

No matter how hard we may try to hide our feelings, the language of our bodies always seems to make our sexual messages perfectly clear! What are the patterns that reveal so much about us?[16]

Courtship readiness

When we're beginning to flirt with the idea of a sexual confrontation, we give ourselves away by our taut muscle tone. The bags around our eyes and that ugly double chin miraculously disappear. Our eyes brighten. We blush or grow pale. Our posture improves and we pull our stomachs in. Our leg muscles tighten. (Think of all the ads you've seen depicting the rugged cowboy leaning coolly against a fence, his pelvis slung forward, his legs apart. A stance designed to sell cigarettes, beer, . . . and sex.)

At the same time, we begin to use "preening" gestures. The aroused woman might stroke her hair, glance at her makeup in the mirror, fuss with her clothing. The aroused man might comb his hair, nervously fidget with his tie, button his coat, and pull up his socks.

These body language signs all combine to say, "I'm interested. Are you?"

Positioning for courtship

The next step involves positioning. There's a singles' bar in New York called Maxwell Plum's. If you sit there for awhile—or in any other singles' bar—you can observe men and women moving unconsciously through an informal mating dance.

These men and women may seem to be simply chatting—talking in a desultory way about Jimmy Carter, charter flights to Europe, or the weather—when, in fact, they're doing much more. If they are attracted to one another, they are deftly arranging and rearranging their bodies in ways that send a clear message to others: "We belong together. This is our territory. Keep out!"

Of course, men and women who are eager to send the opposite message ("I don't belong here. Save me!") unconsciously position themselves quite differently. They gaze longingly at the ceiling or glance distractedly about. They twist their bodies away from their partner toward the larger group. They squirm and shuffle their feet.

Actions of appeal or invitation

Men and women also seduce one another *via* inviting body language. A man may stroll over to a woman's table and gaze at her . . . just a second too long. In response, she might direct flirtatious glances at him or nervously cross her leg, thereby revealing part of her thigh. Her appeal may be as subtle as an exposed wrist or palm, or as blatant as a breast aggressively thrust forward. She might slowly stroke her thigh or wrist; he might loosen his tie or stand closer than he normally would.

HOW DO I LOVE THEE? LET ME COUNT THE WAYS

QUESTION
How *much* do I love him/her?

Psychologists possess an impressive array of techniques for telling how much you love your partner. One psychologist, Zick Rubin, has developed measures of loving and liking. Although he didn't distinguish passionate from companionate love, he did take care to distinguish loving from liking.

"How do I love thee?"

"Let me count the ways."

© 1978 Clarence Brown
in *The Saturday Review*

After all, he observed, "People often express liking for a person whom they would not claim to love in the least. In other instances they may declare their love for someone whom they cannot reasonably be said to like very well."[17]

In order to develop his scales, Rubin sifted through a jumble of lovers', novelists', and scientists' descriptions of love. He concluded that any *love* scale must tap such elements of passion as idealization of the other, tenderness, responsibility, the longing to serve and be served by the loved one, intimacy, the desire to share emotions and experiences, sexual attraction, the exclusive and absorptive nature of the relationship, and, finally, the couple's relative lack of concern with social norms and constraints. Rubin took it for granted that *liking* involved appreciation of the other person, respect, and a feeling that the two of you have a lot in common.

Just for fun, why don't you now try a few items from Rubin's scales. His scales originally contained thirteen items each. On the answer sheet that follows the scales, indicate how you feel about your date, lover, or spouse. Choose the number from 1 ("disagree completely") through 9 ("agree completely") that best represents your feelings about your partner.

Feiffer

© 1975 Jules Feiffer

PASSIONATE LOVE SCALE [18]

1. I feel that I can confide in _____ about virtually everything.

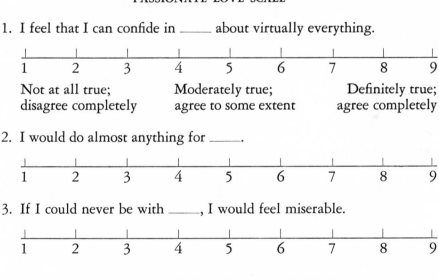

| | | | | | | | | |
|1|2|3|4|5|6|7|8|9|

Not at all true;   Moderately true;   Definitely true;
disagree completely   agree to some extent   agree completely

2. I would do almost anything for _____.

| | | | | | | | | |
|1|2|3|4|5|6|7|8|9|

3. If I could never be with _____, I would feel miserable.

| | | | | | | | | |
|1|2|3|4|5|6|7|8|9|

LIKING/COMPANIONATE LOVE SCALE [18]

1. I think that _____ is unusually well-adjusted.

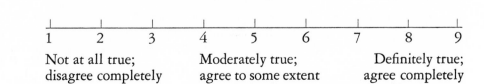

| | | | | | | | | |
|1|2|3|4|5|6|7|8|9|

Not at all true;   Moderately true;   Definitely true;
disagree completely   agree to some extent   agree completely

2. I have great confidence in ___'s good judgment.

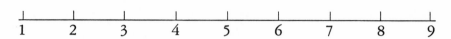

3. ___ is one of the most likable people I know.

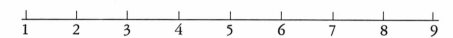

ANSWER SHEET

LOVING SCALE

Your feelings

LIKING SCALE

Your feelings

1. ———————————————————

1. ———————————————————

2. ———————————————————

2. ———————————————————

3. ———————————————————

3. ———————————————————

Now add them all up.

TOTAL:

TOTAL:

You know how you feel about your mate. Would Rubin's items have fairly reflected your feelings? Would he have been able to accurately predict whether you are more "in love" or "in like" with your partner?

Rubin ran the following classified ad in the *University of Michigan Daily:*

> Only dating couples can do it! Gain insight into your relationship by participating in a unique social-psychological study . . . and get paid for it too!

"No, I am not interested in knowing how you would rate me on a scale of one to ten."

Through the ad, Rubin invited young couples who were dating (but not yet engaged) to drop in and complete his liking and love scales. One hundred and fifty-eight couples answered his request. They expressed their feelings on the six liking and love items you filled out, plus twenty more. How did the typical Michigan man or woman feel about his or her date? On the average, college men rated their love for their girlfriends at about 90 points; they rated their liking at about 85 points. Women felt just as intensely about their boyfriends. On the average, college women reported that they loved their boyfriends a total of 89 points and liked them a total of 88 points.

Interestingly enough, in spite of their apparent simplicity, these self-report scales have proven to be surprisingly useful indicators of love and liking. An example: Rubin predicted that men and women who were deeply in love would spend more time gazing into one another's eyes than would more tepid couples. Unbeknownst to the couples, while they were just killing time waiting for the experiment to begin, Rubin carefully recorded how much time they spent gazing into each other's eyes. He found that, as predicted, "strong love" couples spent far more time gazing at one another than did "weak love" couples.

A second example: Six months after the couples had filled out the liking and love scales, Rubin tracked them down to find out what changes, if any, had occurred in their relationships. Which couples were still together? Which had broken up? Which couples' relationships had become more—or less—intense?

Most of the couples' affairs were still surviving. A scattering of the couples were married, more were engaged, most were still going together; only 16 percent of them had broken up. Rubin asked the couples how they thought their relationships were going. Had their affairs become more intense in the last six months? (Sixty percent reported that they had.) Had they stayed about the same? (Nineteen percent felt that the relationship was just where it had been six months before.) Less intense? (Only 21 percent agreed to that. Most of the couples in this category had broken up.)

Rubin found that there was a link between love and courtship progress —but the relationship was a relatively weak one. However, the connection became stronger when Rubin tossed in an extra bit of data.

In his initial interviews, Rubin had noticed that couples seemed to have markedly different ideas about whether or not love and marriage were linked. Some "Romantics" (as Rubin labeled them) believed that "a person should marry whomever he or she loves, regardless of social position" and that "as long as they at least love one another, two people should have no difficulty getting together at marriage." They vehemently disagreed with such statements as: "Economic security should be carefully considered before selecting a marriage partner" or "One should not marry against the serious advice of one's parents." "Nonromantics" were more practical. They insisted that such factors as socioeconomic similarity, personality similarity, and economic security are critical, too.

Rubin predicted that when both partners were Romantics, their love scores should be good predictors of their courtship progress. And they were. When both partners were nonromantics, however, there was no correlation between the couple's love scores and whether their relationship had grown more intense, withered, or had simply maintained the status quo. In fact, the correlation between their love scores and their relationship's progress was actually negative: the higher their love scores, the more likely they were to have broken up six months later.

IN CONCLUSION

We opened the chapter with a question—"What is love anyway?" Apparently, people have very different ideas about love. Some think of it as a pleasurable state; others consider it quite painful. Some feel wildly emotional about it; others think of love simply as a warm attachment to someone else. We'll explore some of these different views in later chapters, but next let's see how people meet each other and fall in love in the first place. As you'll see, the love of your life might be just around the corner.

two
Love: how to find it

*They never met, they never will, for he lived
on the morning side of the mountain and she
lived on the twilight side of the hill.*

Dick Manning and Larry Stock
Morning Side of the Mountain[1]

*I'm a practicing heterosexual . . . but
bisexuality immediately doubles your chances
for a date on Saturday night.*

Woody Allen

THE SEARCH FOR THE BOY—OR GIRL—NEXT DOOR

————•*◊◊◊*•————

QUESTION

Where are all the men and women?

ANSWER

Just around the corner.

————•*◊◊◊*•————

The first step in beginning a love affair is to find someone who's interested. But how do you find that person? Many of us make the mistake of hanging all of our hopes on one (often unobtainable) person.

• Al Hejazy recently moved to Healy Fork, Alaska, to work on the Trans-Alaskan pipeline. He spends all day, every day, sorting out the competing demands of oil experts, geologists, and heavy-equipment operators. So far, the only woman he's gotten to know is an aging Eskimo woman who runs the local coffee shop. Al's hopes rest on the pretty company secretary. He spends hours thinking of ways to elicit her interest.

• Barbara Radke is a young divorcée. She is desperately eager to meet some men. She wants to get married, quit working, and take care of her two small children. But it's hard. Every Friday night she drops in at Topsy's, a singles' bar near where she works. Barbara spends a lot of time trying to figure out what the few men that she *is* interested in want. She tries to be coolly beautiful, yet display a certain gypsy quality; to be aloof, yet passionate; to be nurturant, yet vulnerable. Most Fridays, however, nobody approaches her. Barbara finds the whole thing humiliating. Worse yet, she's spent money on a babysitter and nothing's come of it. She vows she's never coming back—but she does, because she wants to meet some men.

• Nora Kahn has been carrying on a bittersweet affair with a married man for more than two years. John usually drops by early Thursday nights after work. She always has an elegant dinner waiting. After dinner, they rub each other's back, talk, and leisurely make love. Sometimes, often at the last minute, John can't come—he has to go to a Little League game or it's his wife's birthday or he and his wife have theatre tickets. Nora is bitter. She goes round and round: Why doesn't he love her as desperately as she loves him? Why is he so skittish about making any commitment to her?

What these men and women fail to realize is that any time a person's total hopes for happiness depend on the whim of one, or even a few, possible lovers, that person is in trouble. Even if they win, they lose. In every

all about
♥ ♠ LOVE ♥ ♠
by Daisy

Dear Daisy,

I think I've met the perfect man. He's considerate and thoughtful, good-looking, widely-traveled, successful, just the right age—twenty-eight to my twenty-two—has a good sense of humor, and on top of that, he seems to like me (i.e. sent me a valentine after only one date, called me after I'd sprained my ankle on one of our dates to make sure I was OK, always seems extremely glad to see me when he picks me up for a date, etc.).

So what's my problem? He can live without me and it's all too obvious. Perhaps he's playing it cool, but I think two- to three-week intervals between dates add up to too much "cool."

Daisy, this really makes me feel insecure because I don't understand it. I got so desperate last week that I called him and asked him to dinner. He accepted enthusiastically and told me repeatedly that it was nice to hear from me. Well, the dinner was perfect; he was very appreciative and complimentary; he seemed to enjoy everything. But he left with a "See you later."   *Allie*

P.S. I'm positive there isn't another woman in his life, and the problem isn't that he doesn't call but that his calls are too infrequent.

Don't pine away for someone who can live without you. If he can go for two or three weeks without calling, he's not playing it cool; he's just not very interested. See him, but keep your eyes open for someone not so perfect but who finds you irresistible.

case, men and women would do far better if they converted the energy they normally spend on attracting one partner, who may or may not be interested in them, to devising ways to meet twenty potential partners.

Proximity is a critical prerequisite for liking and love. Often, a person's search for the ideal mate ends with the girl or boy next door—or, if he or she is unusually daring, with the girl or boy a mile or two away.

One sociologist interviewed 431 couples at the time they applied for marriage licenses. He found that, at the time of their first date together, 37 percent of the couples were living within eight blocks of one another and 54 percent lived within sixteen blocks of one another. The number of marriages decreased steadily as the distance between the residences increased.[2]

Recently, *Redbook* magazine asked a scattering of celebrities how they had met their match. Interestingly enough, almost all of these eminent men and women—who had "the world" to choose from—somehow ended up with people whom they saw on a day-to-day basis. President Jimmy Carter began by dating the girl next door and ended up marrying the woman down the street; Julia McWilliams Child, the "French chef," met her husband Paul at work. During World War II they were both in the OSS: she was working in Washington, "hoping to become a spy," while Paul was working with the British in India, setting up a war room for Lord Mountbatten. They met when they were both transferred to the same office in Ceylon.

Barbra Streisand met hairdresser Jon Peters at a party in Paris and he offered to do her hair. Streisand observes:

> I made an appointment with him for the following day. I don't usually show up on time for things anyway, and that day I happened to be forty-five minutes late. A big mistake. "Who the hell do you think you are, making me wait forty-five minutes? I don't care what your reputation is or how big a so-called superstar you are. Nobody makes Jon Peters wait." I was surprised. Pleasantly surprised. The man had guts. I liked him immediately. We became friends, then we started going out, and we've been together ever since.[3]

Comedienne Joan Rivers met producer Edgar Rosenberg when he asked her to work with him on a script.

> He was going to the West Indies that weekend to work on still another script. So he took me along. We had to share a cottage. There were two bedrooms with a connecting door. "Aha!" I thought, and started piling things against the door like crazy. Then I heard a sound from his side— the door lock going "click." Well, we were there for four days and when we came back we decided to get married. It all happened so fast that

when we drove up to Larchmont to introduce Edgar to my parents, the chauffeur got out of the limousine first and my parents were all over him.[4]

Psychologist Leon Festinger came up with more solid evidence that people often end up dating and marrying whoever happens to be close by. He examined the development of friendships in a new apartment complex. In the complex, all the apartments, except for the end houses, were arranged around U-shaped courts; the apartments looked out onto a grassy court. The two end houses in each court faced onto the street.

Festinger and his colleagues arrived at the unsettling conclusion that, to a great extent, the architects had unknowingly shaped the social lives of their residents. The major determinant of who became friends was mere proximity—the distance between apartments. Friendships sprung up more frequently between next-door neighbors, less frequently between people

Those residents who are forced, by architectural design, into contact with their neighbors, will be unusually popular. (Reprinted from Walster, Walster, and Berscheid, *Equity Theory and Research,* Boston, Allyn & Bacon, 1978.)

whose houses were separated by another house, and so on. As the distance between houses increased, the number of friendships fell off so rapidly that it was rare to find a friendship between people who lived in houses more than four or five units apart.

Any architectural feature that forced a resident to bump into other residents now and then tended to increase his or her popularity. For example, people with apartments near the entrances and exits of the stairways tended to meet more people and make more friends than did other residents. The residents of the apartments near the mailboxes in each building also had an unusually active social life.

Any architectural feature that took a person even slightly out of the traffic mainstream had a chilling effect on his or her popularity. In order to have the street appear "lived on," ten of the apartments had been turned so that they faced the street, rather than the court. This apparently small change had a considerable effect on the lives of the people who happened to occupy these end houses. These people—who had no next-door neighbors—ended up with less than half as many friends in the complex as anyone else. Architecture had made them involuntary social isolates.[5]

SOME PRACTICAL RECOMMENDATIONS

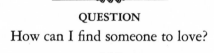

QUESTION
How can I find someone to love?

It's now fairly clear that if you hope to find someone to love, you had better arrange your life so as to have plenty of opportunity to associate with a variety of eligible men or women on a fairly regular basis. Some men and women continually bemoan the fact that eligible partners are in short supply: "Everyone I bump into is married, gay, or on the make." But when friends urge them into activities where they are likely to meet some more eligible partners, they insist they're "too poor," "too tied down," "too busy," or "too something" to come along.

Americans (evidently all subscribing to the myth that one's true love should just happen along) are often fairly shy about admitting they are searching for romantic and sexual partners. There are more avowed Communists, Socialists, and pyromaniacs in the United States than avowed love seekers. Unless desperate, people even shun the once-popular computer matching services—and those desperate enough to subscribe feel compelled to think up excuses for why they're participating ("I'm just doing this on a dare." "I'm looking for a very special kind of woman—the kind I never get a chance to meet in Rawlings, Wyoming.").

Because of this reluctance to be candid about their need for love and sex, men and women interested in contacting a desirable mate must adopt a somewhat devious strategy. They must search for mates while pretending to be doing something else. If dissatisfied with the partners they bump into at school, work, or in the neighborhood, they have the best chance of meeting a wider selection by becoming intensely involved in some activity that "just happens" to bring them into continual contact with potential lovers.

If you really want to find someone to love, you'll have to put some energy into it. There are many ways to begin:

• First, concentrate on making sure you're surrounded by people. Invite the merest of acquaintances to your home for dinner, to a movie, or to a party. Assume that you have to ask first. Don't spend your time longing for the ideal mate. He or she might not be so "ideal" by the third date.

• Be extra friendly to those in the neighborhood, at school, and at work. They're the people most likely to become—or at least to introduce you to—compatible mates.

• Try to get deeply involved in something. Pick an activity you genuinely like. Join a little-theatre group, a snorkeling club devoted to exploring sunken ships, a group that specializes in playing Renaissance festival music, a craft society, or a study group on transsexualism, transvestism, or celibacy. If you insist that you're not interested in anything, you've identified a serious problem. A person who's not interested in anything is not very interesting. If you are at a loss, just pick *any* activity. Hopefully, while you're learning why you hate the oboe, you'll have a chance to encounter some interesting people.

• Even if you're a shy, rather dull person, sheer exposure can work to your advantage. Dr. Robert Zajonc has shown that repeated exposure to anything generates positive feelings for that thing—in other words, mere exposure breeds liking. This process occurs, in part, because we are programmed to evaluate unfamiliar objects negatively. Something unfamiliar is potentially dangerous. Repeated exposure reassures us that the object is not dangerous, so we can relax and respond positively.[6]

If there simply isn't anyone eligible in your neighborhood, at work, or in the activities you like, two other strategies might be helpful. The one you select will depend on how shy or not shy you believe yourself to be. Both work.

IF YOU'RE NOT SHY

You might embark on a fairly flamboyant program if you're not slowed by shyness. In his primers on *How to Pick Up Men!* and *How to Pick Up Girls!,* Eric Weber lists a staggering array of places where men and women

*Repeated exposure to anything generates
positive feelings for that thing.*

commonly encounter suitable dates. There are, of course, the standard ones, like bars, planes, buses, trains, restaurants, museums, beaches, swimming pools, lakes, and parks. But Weber also makes several less obvious suggestions for men:

Visit a library and sit down at the same table as a dynamite girl.

Take a night course in adult school.

Join your local Democratic or Republican club. Or SDS or YAF if you're so disposed.

Pretend you're shopping for a gift for your mother or sister in a fashionable women's clothing store. These places can be real gold-mines, because they're simply crawling with thousands of young, good-looking girls.

Go to church or synagogue. You'll always find single girls at religious services. . . .

Go ice skating or roller skating at a big, crowded rink. Go to dances. In the final analysis, go anywhere where there are lots of girls around. This way you'll vastly increase your chances of picking some up.[7]

Helen Gurley Brown, the editor of *Cosmopolitan,* provides an equally comprehensive list of suggestions for women:

> There are perfectly good ways of making it easy for a man to talk to *you,* which he's probably dying to do but is merely shy. The thing to do is give him something to start a conversation *about.*
>
> Wear a lapel pin with a message printed on it. I'm serious about this. I have three. One says, "I have gray hair, brown eyes and a black heart," and has always been a smash hit.
>
> Once people see writing on you, they won't rest until they've read it. Total strangers will put on glasses to make the grade, and after that, they almost have to say *something* to you not to be rude.
>
> Carry a controversial book at all times—like Karl Marx's *Das Kapital* or *Lady Chatterley's Lover.* It's a perfectly simple way of saying, "I'm open to conversation," without having to start one. . . .
>
> Ride a bicycle to work. Or a Vespa. Be the only girl who walks while everybody else rides.[8]

In Madison, where we live, T-shirt messages are great conversation starters. Elaine's mother sent her one T-shirt which announces boldly, "I don't talk to strangers!" Her sister, Mary—obviously working at cross purposes—sent her a shirt emblazoned with "My body is my own, but I share." Anytime Elaine wears either of these shirts, people inevitably walk up and strike up a conversation.

You can probably come up with some very good ideas of your own. Get a job where the eligible people are: in an all-male or all-female college; in a law school, medical school, college of engineering, or school of home economics; at a military base, or hospital; in a seminary or a church. Canvas for the presidential election, city council race, or the Highway 104 referendum. Visit an airport when planes are socked in. You'll meet businessmen and businesswomen, college students, and vacationers who are dying to talk to someone—for hours. When catastrophe strikes—when there's a power failure, an ice storm, or just a muddy day—organize rescue services—and a party. Locate a dry, warm apartment, get some wine, food, and music together, and sit around in the dark chatting and having fun.

IF YOU'RE SHY

Shyness is a complex and prevalent problem. Philip Zimbardo, a Stanford psychologist, conducted a long-term study of shyness. He found that more

Organize rescue services.

than 40 percent of his subjects considered themselves presently shy; more than 80 percent said they have been shy at some point in their lives. Surprisingly, many celebrities, like Carol Burnett, Barbara Walters, Lawrence Welk, and F. Lee Bailey, are shy. So, the first thing to realize is that you're not alone. In fact, almost half of the people you see every day are shy. Dr. Zimbardo suggests a number of ways to overcome shyness. We've chosen just a few to get you started in feeling more comfortable in social situations.

Saying "hello"

For the next week, greet every person that you pass on the street, in your office, or at school. Smile and say, "Hello, nice day." Since most of us aren't used to being greeted on the street, you may find that many people are surprised when you talk to them. Some may not respond, but in most cases you'll get an equally pleasant response.

Anonymous conversations

A good way to practice your conversational skills is to strike up a *safe* conversation with strangers in public places, like grocery-store lines,

theatre lines, a political rally, the doctor's waiting room, a sports event, the bank, the PTA, church, the library.

Starting a conversation

So there you are in the library or investment course, or at a dinner party or mixer. How do you start a conversation? First of all, choose someone who looks approachable, a person who is smiling at you or sitting alone or wandering around. Don't choose someone who's obviously busy doing something else.

There are a number of ways to start a conversation. Choose the one that is most appropriate to your situation and most comfortable for you.

- Introduce yourself. "Hello, my name is _____." Exchange information on where you live, what you do, your families, etc.

- Give compliments. An easy way to start conversations and to help others (as well as yourself) feel good is to give compliments.

- Request help. Make it obvious you need it and think the other person can provide it.

- Try self-disclosure. You'll find that when you make an obviously personal statement, it will elicit a positive, sympathetic response. Try:

"I'm not sure what I'm doing here, I'm really quite shy." "I just got a divorce and feel a little shakey."

Keeping the conversation flowing

Once you've started a conversation, you can use several techniques to keep it going:

- Ask a question that is either *factual:* "How did the Dodgers do yesterday?" or *personal:* "What do you think of this city council meeting?"
- Offer a personal story or opinion.
- Get the other person talking about himself or herself: "Where did you grow up?" "What kind of work do you do?"
- Express interest in the other person's expertise: "How do you start a day-care center?"
- Most important, share your reactions to what is taking place at that moment while you are interacting. Relate your thoughts and feelings about what the other person has said or done.

Active listening

Become an active listener by paying attention to what people are saying around you. You can pick up a lot of information and clues to personality by listening carefully to conversations or discussion.[8]

Once you've practiced talking to strangers enough so that you feel comfortable doing so, you're ready to plunge into deeper water. Stir up your courage, arrange to meet some eligible men and women, and practice your newly emerging skills on them. Don't worry if something goes wrong. Just try again.

QUESTION
I don't want to be rejected.
Why risk it?

What is the most important determinant of whether a man or woman is popular—or unpopular? Although social assets such as good looks, personality, and money are important, they aren't the most important things. What really seems to be critical is how relaxed a person is about his or her social relations. The people who do best socially are those who are pleased if others like them—but aren't particularly concerned if they don't. The people who do worst are those who are sensitive to rejection. Such people

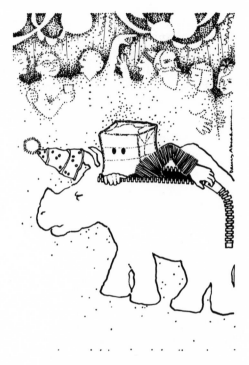

In social situations, sensitivity
is not an asset.

constantly and compulsively assess the other person's degree of interest. And, if by chance they are rejected, they take it extremely hard. In social relations, excessive sensitivity is not an asset.

For example, one very popular man was a master of audacity. In his sophomore year at college, he had dated a girl, been deeply involved with her, and, without a word of explanation, dropped her. A few months later he called her dorm—not to talk to her, but to ask her roommate out. The roommate was enraged. She itemized his faults and slammed down the phone. He called back, saying rather casually, "Well, I guess that means you won't go out with me Friday night. How about Saturday?" The roommate was so taken aback—that she didn't know what to say—so she answered "yes."

Most of us spend enormous amounts of time and energy trying to become an ever-more desirable person—someone whom everyone likes and no one disdains. We'd probably do far better if we simply relaxed and accepted ourselves as we are. That sounds a lot easier than it is, of course, but it's well worth a try. By now you're a well-formed person. You possess some very special talents and, admittedly, a few flaws. Your basic essence is likely to shine through despite tortured efforts to change yourself one way or another. So relax. You're a pretty special person just as you are. So use your energy to meet as many people as possible. Don't worry about the ones who aren't interested in you. They don't count, and you probably wouldn't like them anyway. Look for people who will enjoy *you*.

three
Understanding passionate love

Pains of love be sweeter far
Than all other pleasures are.

John Dryden
Tyrannic Love (1669)

How many ways can you say
"I love you" and mean it?

ANSWER
Six, maybe nine ways
————•❀❀❀•————

When it comes to love, each of us is confident that we know the real thing and we're reluctant to accept other notions. But we often speak different languages when we say, "I love you." Sociologist John Lee asked Americans, Canadians, and Britons to talk about their ideas of love. He found that when lovers say, "I love you," they may mean any of six, or possibly nine, different things[1]:

- Eros: love of beauty
- Mania: obsessive love
- Ludis: playful love
- Storge: companionate love
- Agape: altruistic love
- Pragma: realistic love

Eros. Erotic lovers feel an immediate, powerful attraction to beautiful people. They speak with delight of their lovers' hair, skin, fragrance, muscles, body proportions, and so on.

Erotic lovers are fascinated by every aspect of their beloved. They want to know every detail about them, to become a part of them. They delight in sexual intimacy. Usually, erotic love burns intensely and then dies. Only rarely does the initial rapture blossom into a more lasting love.

Ludis. In the first century A.D., the Roman poet Ovid came up with the concept *amor ludens*—that is, playful love as a game. Ovid advised lovers to enjoy love as a pleasant pastime without getting too deeply ensnared.

Ludis turns love into a series of challenges and puzzles to be solved. Ludic lovers are careful, then, not to become too attached to their partners or to allow their partners to become too dependent on them. They arrange encounters in a casual, even careless, way: "I'll see you around sometime." They date several partners; they keep their lovers dangling. They refuse to mention any long-range plans.

Storge. Storge (pronounced stor-gay) is "love without fever, tumult, or folly, a peaceful and enchanting affection," the kind of feelings you might have for a brother or sister. Storge often sneaks up unobserved: couples begin as friends; they share ideas and activities; they come to enjoy each other more and more. Gradually, their friendship deepens into love. Even if they decide to separate as lovers, they remain good friends. Storge is definitely not the stuff of dramatic plays or romantic novels.

Mania. Lee observes:

> The Greeks called it *theia mania,* the madness from the gods. Both Sappho and Plato, along with legions of sufferers, recorded its symptoms: agitation, sleeplessness, fever, loss of appetite, heartache. The manic lover is consumed by thoughts of the beloved. The slightest lack of enthusiasm from the partner brings anxiety and pain; each tiny sign of warmth brings instant relief, but no lasting satisfaction. The manic lover's need for attention and affection from the beloved is insatiable. Cases of mania abound in literature, for its components—furious jealousy, helpless obsession, and tragic endings—are the stuff of human conflict. . . .
>
> The manic lover alternates between peaks of ecstasy when he feels loved in return, and depths of despair when the beloved is absent.[2]

Pragma. Pragma lovers take a practical approach to love. From the first, they are on the lookout for the right match—someone whose personality, background, education, religious views, interests, and the like will be compatible with their own. Computer dating services are based on the pragma philosophy. Once a sensible choice is made, more intense feelings may develop.

Agape. Agape (pronounced ah-ga-pay) is the classical Christian form of love—love that is patient, kind, and never demands reciprocity. St. Paul, in his letters to the Corinthians, wrote that Christians have a duty to care about others, whether the others are deserving of their love or not. All the great religions share this concept of love.
Lee admits:

> I found no saints in my sample. I have yet to interview an unqualified example of agape, although a few respondents had brief agapic episodes in relationships that were otherwise tinged with selfishness. For instance, one of my subjects, seeing that his lover was torn between choosing him or another man, resolved to save her the pain of deciding; he bowed out gracefully. His action fell short of pure agape, however, because he continued to be interested in how well his beloved was doing, and was

purely and selfishly delighted when she dropped the other man and re-turned to him.[3]

Three other kinds of love—mixtures of the more basic types—may be added to those we've discussed: Storgic-Eros, Ludic-Eros, and Storgic-Ludis. Each combines attributes of two of the "pure" love forms.

Lee claims that "the way to have a mutually satisfying love affair is to find a partner who shares the same approach to loving, the same definition of love." The farther apart two types of lovers are on the chart, the less likely they are to share a common language about love.

What kind of lover are you? Lee provides a test (see pp. 42–43) to help you see how well matched in attitudes you are with your lover. Remember to look for overall patterns in your experience. Some people have enjoyed a variety of love experiences, but most of us prefer one type.

OUR NOTIONS ABOUT LOVE

QUESTION

Where do we get our ideas about love?

Although our ideas of what we should feel in a certain situation generally determine what we do feel, when it comes to love, most of us aren't quite certain what it is we should feel. Our ideas about love are often quite jumbled. Where did we get these notions?

IT STARTS WITH OUR CULTURE

Anthropologists insist that, in some primitive societies, passionate love doesn't even exist. When one anthropologist asked the Tahitians to describe their passionate feelings, they were incredulous. They'd never heard of anyone feeling like *that*. Was such a person, they wondered, mad?[5]

In most cultures, however, it's simply taken for granted that, sooner or later, everyone falls in love. We are obedient; we do. Several decades ago anthropologist Ralph Linton made this rather harsh observation:

> All societies recognize that there are occasional violent emotional attach-ments between persons of the opposite sex, but our present American culture is practically the only one which has attempted to capitalize on these and make them the basis for marriage. The hero of the modern American movie is always a romantic lover, just as the hero of an old Arab epic is always an epileptic. A cynic may suspect that in any ordinary

population the percentage of individuals with capacity for romantic love of the Hollywood type was about as large as that of persons able to throw genuine epileptic fits.[6]

By their late teens, 97 percent of American men and women have fallen in love . . . often more than once.

Not only does our culture tell us that love exists, it also gives us a rough idea as to when it's appropriate to feel love and when it isn't. From "Snow White," "Cinderella," and "The Princess and the Frog"—and later on from *True Romance* and *Argosy*—we learn that if we are just beautiful and sweet enough, or handsome and rugged enough, a handsome prince or beautiful princess will chance along and change our lives. From the *Feminine Mystique* and *The Male Machine* and our consciousness-raising groups, we learn that maybe he or she won't.

From the sunny lyrics of "Afternoon Delight" or "Almost Like Being in Love," we learn that love is a positive experience—one associated with euphoria, sexual ecstasy, excitement, and joy. From the down-and-out lyrics of "Can't Help Lovin' dat Man," we learn that love is a painful experience —one inexorably linked to sexual deprivation, longing for appreciation, and the shame of rejection and neglect.

Movies, television, gothic novels, "As The World Turns," "Mary Hartman, Mary Hartman," *The Reader's Digest,* and *Playboy* all promote their particular notions of love. In general, our ideas as to what love is come from this jumble of impressions. No wonder, then, that we find love confusing!

IT CONTINUES IN THE FAMILY

In childhood we painstakingly learn—either by observation or by adult direction—what emotions are appropriate in which situations. We learn when to feel joyful or sad, fearful or secure, excited or bored.

The child's world is an emotionally confusing one. Imagine, for example, this scene: A little boy is playing quietly with his truck. The doorbell rings; his mother rushes to the door to greet a friend and her infant daughter. The little boy watches. He rubs his eyes; he has missed his nap. Soon it will be dinner time; he experiences vague hunger pangs. While absorbed in the visitors' movements, he accidentally runs his truck over his hand; it hurts. He watches his mother talking and gesturing to the visitor and her little girl. Her voice seems unusually high and animated. They all look at him. His nose tickles.

In response to this complex of factors, the boy becomes momentarily overwrought. He hides his face in his mother's skirt for a few seconds, and then peers out. What caused him to hide his face? What emotion is he

GRAPH YOUR OWN STYLE OF LOVING⁴

Consider each characteristic as it applies to a current relationship that you define as love, or to a previous one if that is more applicable. For each, note whether the trait is *almost always true* (AA), *usually true* (U), *rarely true* (R), or *almost never true* (AN).

No.	Characteristic	Responses (in order shown)
1	You consider your childhood less happy than the average of peers.	R, AN, U
2	You were discontent with life (work, etc.) at time your encounter began.	R, AN, U
3	You have never been in love before this relationship.	R
4	You want to be in love or have love as security.	R, AN, AA, U
5	You have a clearly defined ideal image of your desired partner.	AA, AN, AN, AA
6	You felt a strong gut attraction to your beloved on the first encounter.	AA, R, AN, R
7	You are preoccupied with thoughts about the beloved.	AA, AN, AN, AA
8	You believe your partner's interest is at least as great as yours.	U, R, AN, U
9	You are eager to see your beloved almost every day; this was true from the beginning.	AA, AN, R, AA, R
18	You lose ability to be first to terminate relationship.	AN, AN, AA, R
19	You try to force beloved to show more feeling, commitment.	AN, AN, AA
20	You analyze the relationship, weigh it in your mind.	AN, U, AA
21	You believe in the sincerity of your partner.	AA, AN, U
22	You blame partner for difficulties of your relationship.	R, U, R, U
23	You are jealous and possessive to the point of angry conflict.	U, AN, R
24	You are jealous to the point of conflict, scenes, threats, etc.	AN, AN, AN, AA, AN
25	Tactile, sensual contact is very important to you.	AA, AN, AN, R
26	Sexual intimacy was achieved early, rapidly in the relationship	AA, AN, AN, AN
27	You take the quality of sexual rapport as a test of love.	AA, U, AN, R

	Eros	Ludus	Storge	Mania	Pragma
28 You are willing to work out sex problems, improve technique.	U	R	R	R	U
29 You have a continued high rate of sex tactile contact throughout the relationship.	U	R	R	R	R
30 You declare your love first, well ahead of partner.	AA	AN	AN	AA	R
31 You consider love life your most important activity, even essential.	AA	AN	R	AA	R
32 You are prepared to "give all" for love once under way.	U	AN	U	AA	R
33 You are willing to suffer abuse, even ridicule from partner.	AN	AN	R	AA	AN
34 Your relationship is marked by frequent differences of opinion, anxiety.	R	AA	R	AA	R
35 The relationship ends with lasting bitterness, trauma for you.	AN	R	R	AA	R

	Eros	Ludus	Storge	Mania	Pragma
10 You soon believed this could become a permanent relationship.	AA	AN	R	AN	U
11 You see "warning signs" of trouble but ignore them.	R	R	R	AA	R
12 You deliberately restrain frequency of contact with partner.	AN	AA	R	R	
13 You restrict discussion of your feelings with beloved.	R	AA	U	U	U
14 You restrict display of your feelings with beloved.	R	AA	R	U	U
15 You discuss future plans with beloved.	AA	R	R		AA
16 You discuss wide range of topics, experiences with partner.	AA	R			AA
17 You try to control relationship, but feel you've lost control.	AN	AN	AN	AA	

To diagnose your style of love, look for patterns across characteristics. If you consider your childhood less happy than that of your friends, were discontent with life when you fell in love, and very much want to be in love, you have "symptoms" that are rarely typical of eros and almost never true of storge, but which do suggest mania. Where a trait did not especially apply to a type of love, the space in that column is blank. Storge, for instance, is not the *presence* of many symptoms of love, but precisely their absence. It is cool, abiding affection rather than *Sturm und Drang*.

feeling? Is he afraid of strangers? Is he playing a game? Is he angry because the truck hurt his hand? Is he trying to get attention? Is he jealous of the little girl?

His mother provides an answer. She says, "Don't be shy, John. Susan won't hurt you. Come out and meet her." His mother reduces a chaotic jumble of stimuli to manageable size. She teaches him that it is Susan who is causing his emotional agitation. She informs him that, when one has an emotional reaction in the presence of strangers, it is called "shyness." She also communicates to John that the other stimuli—his sore hand, for example—are not responsible for his aroused state.

But parents rarely give us any direct instruction about the nature of love. No mother ever says to her child: "I think you're probably deeply in love with Mrs. Glass," or, "You know what you're feeling? You're feeling sexy, that's what." Parents simply assume that ("Thank God") children don't have feelings like that—or, if they do, it's better not to talk about them.

So, we pick up our families' ideas about the nature of love and sex almost by osmosis. We quietly observe what our parents say and what they do. We listen to the advice our mother gives our sobbing Aunt Bessie when

Parents simply assume ("Thank God")
that children don't have feelings like that.

she says her Jim is seeing another woman. We watch our parents kiss, hug, and touch—or fail to touch—one another.

Most of these ideas we can't even put into words. They come from the shadowy world of childhood—where fantasy is mixed with fact, where events are only dimly perceived, where everything is terribly confusing, and where there's no way to check on our perceptions by asking. Our early ideas may be hazy and confused, but they're etched deeply into our minds. Thus, throughout our lives, they have a profound impact on our notions about love.

IT ENDS WITH OUR OWN EXPERIENCES

Finally, our own romantic experiences have a special impact on how we think about love. Most of us, however, don't have very many romantic experiences. One sociologist who interviewed more than a thousand men and women, ranging in age from eighteen to twenty-four, found that they generally had started dating at about age thirteen.

"When," he asked, "did you first become infatuated with someone?" He found that boys and girls first fell in love with love sometime during their thirteenth year. When did they actually fall in love? Much later—when they were about seventeen. The sociologist also asked men and women how much romantic experience they'd had—how many times they'd fallen in love. The vast majority of men and women reported that they'd fallen in love only once. (On the average, men fall in love 1.2 times; women, 1.3 times.)[7] The average woman receives only two proposals of marriage in a lifetime—and she accepts one.

Our romantic experience is limited—but potent—and, for good or ill, it greatly influences our ideas about love.

MEN AND WOMEN IN LOVE

—•◊◊◊•—

QUESTION

Who's more capable of love—men or
women?
Is there a difference in the way they
experience love?

—•◊◊◊•—

According to folklore, women are the romantics. In country and western songs, it's the woman who plaintively sings of sacrificing everything to be with the man she loves ("Midnight Train to Georgia"), who resolutely "stands by her man" through thick and thin. Men's feelings are less urgent,

"I loved and lost, and married Ed."

Published by Chronicle Books,
San Francisco

more muted: sometimes they're drifters ("Baby, Baby Don't Get Hooked on Me"); sometimes they're solid men beaten down by life's searing experiences ("Sixteen Tons"). But, regardless, they brush aside their passionate or tender emotions.

Theorists of every political persuasion have assumed that the cultural stereotype—women fall in love; men work—has a ring of truth. Aristotle argued that, by nature, men are superior in every respect to women. Not only are they superior in body and mind, but even in the ability to live on via the next generation. (Aristotle erroneously believed that semen transmitted the soul to the embryo. "Feminine secretions" transmitted only an earthly body to the next generation.) "Ergo," Aristotle argued, "because the wife is inferior to her husband, she ought to love him more than he her; algebraically, this would compensate for their inequality and result in a well-balanced relationship." For Aristotle, the "fact" that women are romantics and men are practical is writ in their genes (or rather, in their "semen" and "secretions").[8]

Interestingly enough, modern feminists have tended to agree with Aristotle—that is, they too view women as the more romantic of the two sexes. Shulamith Firestone, in *The Dialectic of Sex: The Case for a Feminist Revolution,* observes, "Men can't love." She finds psychoanalyst Theodor Reik's ideas about the nature of love as compelling as we do. (You'll remember that Reik argued that we all long to be special. When we are made painfully aware that we're not, we begin to cast around for someone who is. We feel that by loving someone, by merging with someone who is perfect, we might somehow share their perfection.) Firestone argues that our patriarchal society brands women "inferiors" from the very first. Thus, it is women who endlessly search for a perfect lover. She comments:

> That women live for love and men live for work is a truism . . . Men were thinking, writing, and creating, because women were pouring their energies into those men; women . . . are preoccupied with love.[9]

Firestone, of course, does not argue that women should cease being lovers. She merely argues that men and women must become equals, so they can both love.

Recently, a few sociologists have asked men and women about their love relationships; their findings have cast doubt on the stereotype of men as passionless lovers. Men appear to fall in love more quickly and to cling more tenaciously to a dying affair than do women. However, men will admit to fewer of the "symptoms" of love than will women.

WHO SAYS MEN AREN'T ROMANTICS?

If you'd like to believe men are the real romantics, here is some evidence to support your argument. In 1958, sociologist Charles Hobart set out to determine whether men or women had the most romantic view of human encounters. Hobart developed the following scale to tap romanticism. He asked 923 men and women to respond to the items. How do you feel about the statements? .

ROMANTICISM SCALE [10]

		Agree	Disagree
*	1. Lovers ought to expect a certain amount of disillusionment after marriage.	____	____
*	2. True love should be suppressed in cases where its existence conflicts with the prevailing standards of morality.	____	____
	3. To be truly in love is to be in love forever.	____	____

* 4. The sweetly feminine "clinging vine" girl   _____ _____
cannot compare with the capable and sym-
pathetic girl as a sweetheart.

5. As long as they at least love each other, two   _____ _____
people should have no trouble getting along
together in marriage.

6. A girl should expect her sweetheart to be   _____ _____
chivalrous on all occasions.

7. A person should marry whomever he loves   _____ _____
regardless of social position.

8. Lovers should freely confess everything of   _____ _____
personal significance to each other.

* 9. Economic security should be carefully con-   _____ _____
sidered before selecting a marriage partner.

* 10. Most of us could sincerely love any one of   _____ _____
several people equally well.

11. A lover without jealousy is hardly to be de-   _____ _____
sired.

* 12. One should not marry against the serious ad-   _____ _____
vice of one's parents.

What's your romanticism score? If you agreed with items 3, 5, 7, 8, or 11 (the items without an asterisk), give yourself one point per item. If you disagreed with items 1, 2, 4, 9, 10, or 12 (the items with an asterisk), give yourself one point per item. Record your total score here _____.

Hobart found that men had a considerably more romantic view of male-female relationships than did women. On the average, women agreed with about four of the romanticism items; on the average, men agreed with more—about five of them.

More ammunition: A group of sex researchers interviewed 700 young lovers. They asked the men and women to tell them a little bit about the person they were in love with right now. (If they weren't in love with anybody right now, the scientists asked them to talk about the last time they were in love.) "How early," they asked, "did you become aware that you loved the other?" The scientists found that while 20 percent of the men fell in love before the fourth date, only 15 percent of the women fell in love that early. At the other extreme, only 30 percent of the men, but a full 43 percent of the women, were not sure if they were in love or not by the twentieth date.[11]

Thus, it appears that men, not women, are the most vulnerable to love. Women are far more cautious about getting involved. There is also solid evidence that it is men who cling the most tenaciously to an obviously stricken affair and who suffer most when it finally dies.

A group of Harvard scientists got acquainted with 231 Boston couples and charted the course of their affairs for two years. They found that, usually, the women decided whether and when an affair should end; the men seemed to stick it out to the bitter end. When things finally did die down, it was the men who suffered the most. The men felt most depressed, most lonely, least happy, and least free after a breakup. They found it extremely hard to accept the fact that they were no longer loved; that the affair was over and there was nothing they could do about it. They were plagued with the hope that if only they said the right thing . . . did the right thing . . . things would be as they were. Women were far more resigned and, thus, were better able to pick up the pieces of their lives and move on.[12]

Interestingly enough, the researchers' contention that it is the men who suffer most when an affair flickers out is consistent with the fact that three times as many men as women commit suicide after a disastrous love affair.

BUT AREN'T WOMEN THE REAL ROMANTICS?

For those of you who'd like to continue to believe that it's women who are the true romantics, we must admit that there is also evidence to support that notion. Simone de Beauvoir observed: "The word love has by no means the same sense for both sexes, and this is one cause of the serious misunderstandings which divide them." [13]

The data suggest that she was right. Researchers asked men and women to describe how they felt when they were in love. To what extent did they experience these love reactions:[14]

- Felt like I was floating on a cloud
- Felt like I wanted to run, jump, and scream.
- Had trouble concentrating.
- Felt giddy and carefree.
- Had a general feeling of well-being.
- Was nervous before dates.
- Had physical sensations: cold hands, butterflies in the stomach, tingling spine, etc.
- Had insomnia.

The lovers were asked to rate their feelings on the following scale:

☐ None
☐ Slight
☐ Moderate
☐ Strong
☐ Very strong

This time, it was the women who appeared to be the romantics. They generally experienced the symptoms of love with some intensity. Men did not. (The one exception: Men and women were both nervous before dates.)

The evidence, then, makes it clear that there is no simple answer to the question: Who are the *real romantics*—men or women? Men tend to fall in love more quickly and cling to a faltering love more tenaciously than do women. However, while the relationship is at its most intense, women experience the euphoria and the agony of love more intensely than do men.

These findings actually do make a certain amount of sense. Traditionally, it is the man who has official initiation privileges: he calls, invites, pursues, proposes. It is the woman who gets invited or proposed to; rarely is she able to select a man overtly. Thus, it's not so surprising to find that the man feels free to plunge headlong after the woman he wants. Nor is it surprising that the woman is very cautious about openly displaying her feelings.

Women might be cautious about rushing headlong into a relationship for another reason as well. As one shrewd observer noted: "There is this difference between the man and the woman in the pattern of bourgeois family life: a man, when he marries, chooses a companion and perhaps a helpmate, but a woman chooses a companion and at the same time a standard of living. It is necessary for a woman to be mercenary."[15]

Feminist Arlie Hochschild agrees. She contends that men and women differ markedly in their willingness to attend to feelings of various kinds, in how they prefer to label their feelings, and—most important—in how hard they try to manage their thoughts and feelings. She finds that women spend a great deal of time trying to feel what they "ought" to feel and trying not to feel what they think they ought not to feel.

Consider, for example, one woman's description of an attempt to make herself love another:

Since we both were somewhat in need of a close man-woman relationship and since we were thrown together so often (we lived next door to each other and it was summertime), I think that we convinced ourselves that we loved each other. *I had to try to convince myself that I loved him* in order to justify or to somehow "make right" sleeping with him. (Which I never really wanted to do.) We ended up living together supposedly because we "loved" each other but I would say instead that we did it for other reasons which neither of us wanted to admit. What pretending I loved him when I really didn't means to me was having a "secret" nervous breakdown.[16]

Or consider this example:

Last summer I was going out with a guy often and began to feel very strongly about him. I knew though that he had just broken up with a girl a year ago because she had gotten too serious about him. So I was afraid to show any emotion. I also was afraid of being hurt, *so I attempted to change* my feelings. *I talked myself into not caring* about Mike . . . but I must admit it didn't work for too long. To sustain this feeling *I had to almost invent bad things about him and concentrate on them or continue to tell myself he didn't care.* It was a *hardening of emotions* I'd say. It took a lot of work and was unpleasant, because I had to concentrate on anything I could find that was irritating about him. (The story does have a happy ending—I finally, after three months, let down my wall and admitted how I felt, and to my surprise and joy, he felt the same way. Things are now going *very* well.)[17]

Men are far less likely to become so absorbed in monitoring and controlling their emotions; they simply feel what they feel. Women, however, try at least to temper their feelings according to the situation. Before the man commits himself to a relationship, the woman tends to play down her feelings. Once she is fairly sure that he is interested in her, she feels free to express fully—if not exaggerate—her love for him. But, she remains ever attentive to his feelings. If she senses that his love for her is fading, she begins to conceal her feelings once again.

LOVE VERSUS INFATUATION

————◆◊◊◆————

QUESTION

How can I tell if I'm *really* in love . . . or
just infatuated?

————◆◊◊◆————

In movies, lovers never have any trouble telling whether or not they're in love. Intense passion stalks them, shakes them around, and—struggle as they might—overwhelms them. In real life, we're usually not so certain about our feelings. Judith Viorst had this wry response to the question: What is the difference between infatuation and love?

> Infatuation is when you think that he's as sexy as Robert Redford, as smart as Henry Kissinger, as noble as Ralph Nader, as funny as Woody Allen and as athletic as Jimmy Connors. Love is when you realize that he's as sexy as Woody Allen, as smart as Jimmy Connors, as funny as Ralph Nader, as athletic as Henry Kissinger and nothing like Robert Redford in any category—but you'll take him anyway.[18]

College students at three universities were asked what one thing they most wished they knew about romantic love. A surprisingly frequent question was: "What is the difference between love and infatuation?"

The solution to the love-versus-infatuation riddle seems to be, quite simply, that there is no difference. Psychologists have become increasingly skeptical that passionate love and infatuation differ in any way—*at the time one is experiencing them.* Two sex counselors who interviewed young adults about their romantic and sexual experiences concluded that the difference between passionate love and infatuation is merely semantic. Lovers use the term "romantic love" to describe loving relationships that are still

This peculiar posture was discovered by Dr. Tithridge in a patient who for thirty years, boy and man, had been unable to tell love from passion and who allowed it to prey on his mind. Drawings from the Tithridge collection of American male postures.

in progress. They use the term "infatuation" to describe once-loving relationships that, for a variety of reasons, were terminated.[19]

It appears, then, that it may be possible to tell infatuation from romantic love only in retrospect. If a relationship flowers, we continue to believe we are experiencing true love; if a relationship dies, we conclude that we were merely infatuated. We need not assume, then, that, at the time we are experiencing the feeling, true love differs in any way from the supposed counterfeit—i.e., infatuation.

QUESTION

If passionate love and infatuation are
exactly the same thing, how come my
mother—and my friends—keep insisting
they can tell the difference?

When deciding whether or not to get involved with someone, you're really faced with two separate questions: Do I love the other person? Is that person right for me?

When our parents and friends grudgingly admit that maybe we are feeling the real thing or vehemently insist that we're not—that we're just "infatuated"—they're not really commenting on our feelings. Actually they're telling us whether or not they approve of our relationship. If they approve of the relationship, they are likely to agree that this may well be love—only time will tell. If they don't approve, they are likely to insist that it's only infatuation—here today, gone tomorrow.

But *you* shouldn't get confused trying to make nonexistent distinctions between the two. It's exciting to come to deeply understand yourself and your emotions. It's important to realize that you love someone and to bask in that feeling, even though you are also painfully aware that the relationship can come to nothing.

QUESTION

How can I tell if the person I love
loves me?

Usually lovers don't try to hide their feelings: they tell their beloved, their friends, strangers on the bus, and the guy at the newsstand how they feel. Even if they're too shy to come right out and say they're in love, their behavior usually gives them away.

In Chapter 1, we described how people indirectly signal that they're in love: eye contact, inclination, how close they stand to each other. Men and women in love also tend to give themselves away in several other ways. First, lovers tend to exaggerate their partners' virtues and minimize their faults—love *is* a little blind. Further, they are deeply involved emotionally; they want to share their emotions and experiences with those they love. Lovers treat their partners tenderly, kindly, and responsibly. And, they are *very* drawn to them sexually.[20]

But some of us often miss these seemingly obvious signals from our partners. Why? Psychologists find that our own feelings about ourselves —whether we basically respect ourselves or have dark misgivings—inevitably color our judgments of how others feel about us. Men and women who have unusually high self-esteem versus unusually low self-esteem react in very different ways to admiration and criticism. High-self-esteem men and women thoroughly relish praise—but they conveniently manage to misperceive, refute, or forget criticism. Low-self-esteem men and women are just the opposite. They are forever on the alert for criticism. They recognize it, accept it, and remember it long, long after.[21]

We are all very adept at protecting our egos. Even if we're wildly interested in someone, we start out by making a few tentative probes to find out where that person stands. We carefully observe how the man or woman we're interested in reacts—and only then do we decide whether or not it's worthwhile to pursue things.

High-self-esteem people are quick to recognize when others are interested in them and quick to decide whether or not to reciprocate. Low-self-esteem people are not. They tend to miss subtle signals of interest. Some, in fact, have such painfully low self-esteem that it warps their judgment.

An example: I once had a college friend who had great misgivings about herself. She worried that she was ugly, that she had bad skin, that

MISS PEACH   By Mell Lazarus

MISS PEACH by Mell Lazarus.
Courtesy of Mell Lazarus and
Field Newspaper Syndicate.

her ankles were fat—that, really, it would be hard for any man to like her. She was steadily dating a man who *said* he liked her—but she wasn't sure. "He never wants to be seen with me in public," she complained. "All he wants to do is lie around his apartment, listening to records and making love. He doesn't love me—he just wants cheap sex." And she'd cry. On her birthday, she went out with him again—and again came home crying. What had happened? He'd taken her to a fraternity dinner-dance and, when he'd dropped her off that night, he'd only given her a light peck goodnight. "He's just trying to ease me out," she moaned. "He doesn't even think I'm sexy any more." (It's not quite clear what he could have done to convince her that he loved her.)

Think about it. Are you set for rejection? Do you tend to interpret the behavior of others in such a way that, no matter what they do, you take it as clear-cut evidence that they don't *really* love you? If so, quit it!

There are, of course, times when your partner may have ambivalent feelings about you. He or she just isn't sure that this is the real thing.

QUESTION

What can I do to inspire feelings of love?

ANSWER

Take it for granted that you're loved.

Probably one of the most effective ways to convince someone who is unsure of his or her feelings for you is to act as if you are more confident of the person's love than you really are. Our ideas about ourselves—and the world—are contagious. When we're feeling good and are convinced that we're irresistible, we somehow manage to convince everyone else as well.

Humorist Dan Greenberg, in *How to Make Yourself Miserable,* observes that one surefire way to destroy a budding relationship is to keep questioning your lover's motivation.

---

*Relationship-destroying maneuver
number one: the great love test*

This maneuver can be used at any stage of a deep relationship, but it seems particularly well suited to the beginning stages of a romance, so we recommend it as your first major stratagem.

This maneuver, as well as the ones that follow, are, of course, based on the reject-me formula.

Reject-me move #1:

You: "Do you love me?"
Mate: "Yes, *of course* I love you."

Reject-me move #2:

You: "Do you *really* love me?"
Mate: "Yes, I really love you."
You: "You really really love me?"
Mate: "Yes, I really really love you."
You: "You're *sure* you love me—you're absolutely sure?"
Mate: "Yes, I'm absolutely sure."
        (*pause*)
You: "Do you know the meaning of the word love?"
        (*pause*)
Mate: "I don't know."
You: "Then how can you be so sure you love me?"
        (*pause*)
Mate: "I don't know. Perhaps I can't."

Reject-me move #3:

You: "You can't, eh? I see. Well, since you can't even be sure you love
        me, I can't really see much point in our remaining together. Can you?
        (*pause*)
Mate: "I don't know. Perhaps not."
        (*pause*)
You: "You've been leading up to this for a pretty long time, haven't you?"[22]

Thus, high-self-esteem people have a second, continuing advantage
over their low-esteem counterparts. Secure men and women are quick to
perceive—and respond to—their lovers' expressions of affection. Insecure
men and women aren't. Even when their lovers tell them they love them,
they remain skeptical. They ask for reassurance. Or, worse yet, they argue
with their lovers: "You don't love me. If you loved me, you wouldn't
treat me this way." In the end, they usually win their case.

four
The delightful side
of passionate love

I believe myself that romantic love is the source of the most intense delights that life has to offer. In the relation of a man and a woman who love each other with passion and imagination and tenderness, there is something of inestimable value, to be ignorant of which is a great misfortune to any human being.

Bertrand Russell
Marriage and Morals

Observers disagree, passionately, about the types of emotional experiences that are most likely to fuel passion. Most insist that passionate love is inexorably intertwined with joy and fulfillment. A few insist that passionate love and agony are virtually synonymous. (Indeed, the original meaning of passion *was* agony—as in Christ's passion.) Social psychologists would argue that both intense joy and intense suffering can contribute to passion. Both intensely joyous and intensely painful experiences are physiologically arousing: reassurance, sexual pleasure, challenge, and excitement are arousing, as are anxiety, fear, frustration, jealousy, anger, and total confusion. Under the right conditions, both joy and anguish should have the potential for deepening passion.

Is there any evidence to support this contention? Yes. In this chapter, we explore the dazzling side of love and discuss how the delight we share with others helps kindle our passion. In Chapter 5, we look at the darker side of love. As we learn there, it's sometimes possible to love others passionately not *in spite* of the suffering they cause us, but *because* of it.

LOVE: THE FANTASY

Lovers often fall desperately in love with someone they barely know. Crazy? Not really. When we close our eyes and daydream, it's easy to summon up a flawless lover—a man or woman who instantaneously satisfies all our unspoken, fleeting, extravagant, and conflicting desires. Once we get to know someone, of course, our reactions are far more tepid; it becomes evident that he or she is certainly not the stuff of our dreams. In an interview with Curtis Bill Pepper, Marcello Mastroianni made the following observation.

––––––––––•*0-0-0*•––––––––––

I lack the capabilities of real, serious love. I try, but I always fail. You know why? We spoke of the nature of the actor, his need to exalt everything, even a woman, to mythicize her so that she becomes an object in another adventure. You desire her in an imaginary, almost literary sense, taking away all that's human.

That's my trouble. I believe I'm having a great love, but it's only on a plane of fantasy. I can't bring it down to the acts, the gestures, the attitudes of one who's really in love. Maybe one should love without imagining too much. But I can't, and it becomes a game where I'm left with the fantasy while the reality, the woman I love, is eventually gone. So you see how the fantasy of an actor, when removed from the stage, is really his enemy, destroying any chance he has for a normal, happy life.

In "Mastroianni Talks about Real-Life
Love," *Vogue,* October 1977, p. 122.
Copyright © 1977 by Condé Nast
Publications, Inc.

––––––––––•*0-0-0*•––––––––––

Think back to our discussion of Freud in Chapter 1. We suggested then that, throughout their lives, men and women continue to long for the total love and fulfillment they once had as infants. Scientists really have no compelling explanation as to why men and women so relentlessly continue to hope that, through love, they will attain the unattainable. But we agree that they do. While our faith in a specific lover may well be extinguished by a disillusioning experience, our love affair with love is not even dampened. We continue to assure ourselves that *next time* things will be different—*next time* we'll find that fantasied lover, who will bring us total fulfillment.

The fantasy that the person we love is about to make our lives complete, then, is one primitive fuel for romantic passion.

THE GREATER OUR NEED, THE MORE GRANDIOSE OUR FANTASIES

Sigmund Freud claimed that "happy people never make fantasies, only unsatisfied ones do." [1] Psychoanalyst Theodor Reik elaborated on Freud's argument by suggesting that when people are most unhappy with themselves and their lives, they are most vulnerable to love:

> In the ordinary person there is only a general ill-contested feeling of restlessness or impatience, an indefinite mood, sometimes boredom or loneliness, a distaste or even dislike of oneself, a sense of incompleteness and nostalgia, a desire to belong. . . . It is as if a voice deep inside himself were saying, "There is something amiss or missing." [2]

It is *then* that violent passion springs up. As Dorothy Parker observed:

SYMPTOM RECITAL

I do not like my state of mind:
I'm bitter, querulous, unkind.
I hate my legs, I hate my hands,
I do not yearn for lovelier lands.
I dread the dawn's recurrent light;
I hate to go to bed at night.
I snoot at simple, earnest folk.
I cannot take the gentlest joke.
I find no peace in paint or type.
My world is but a lot of tripe.
I'm disillusioned, empty-breasted.
For what I think, I'd be arrested.
I am not sick, I am not well.

My quondam dreams are shot to hell.
My soul is crushed, my spirit sore;
I do not like me any more.
I cavil, quarrel, grumble, grouse.
I ponder on the narrow house.
I shudder at the thought of men . . .
I'm due to fall in love again.[3]

Social psychologists have found some evidence that the psychoanalysts are right. Acute deprivation *does* seem to set the stage for passionate fantasies. When we can't have what we want, we often dream about getting it. With two colleagues,[4] we decided to test this simple hypothesis: When we're sexually aroused, our minds wander, and pretty soon our dazzling fantasies lend sparkle to drab reality.

First, one of our group contacted a number of college men. He identified himself as a staff member of the Center for Student Life Studies and explained that the Center was studying the dating practices of college students. He told each subject that they'd like to know how he felt about a blind date they'd picked out for him. Would he participate? Most of the men said, "Sure."

While the men sat around waiting to give their first impressions of their date-to-be, they whiled away the time by reading articles lying around the office. This material was carefully selected. One group of men was given fairly boring reading material, articles intended to make the subjects cool and calm. The second group was given *Playboy*-type material, designed to make them very "hot."

Finally, the interviewer returned. He showed the men a picture of their date (a fairly attractive blond coed) and told them a little about her. (She seemed to be fairly intelligent, easy to get along with, active, and moderately liberal.) What did the men think of her? Well, that depended on what they had been reading.

We proposed that an unaroused man should be a pretty objective man; his fantasy life is in "low gear" and it's easy for him to take women as they are. An aroused man should have a harder time of it; the luster of his daydreams should keep rubbing off on his date-to-be. When a man is feeling sexy, he should have a greater tendency to see women as sex objects; thus, he should tend to exaggerate two of his date's traits: (1) her sexual desirability, and (2) her sexual receptivity.

We found we were right. As predicted, the more aroused a man was, the more beautiful he thought his date was. In addition, the more aroused he was, the more likely he was to assume that his date would be sexually receptive. Unaroused men judged their date-to-be to be a fairly nice girl. Aroused men suspected that she was probably a fairly "amorous," "immoral," "promiscuous," "willing," "unwholesome," and uninhibited girl. (This finding gives us a new insight into the rapist's claim that "she asked for it.")

THE FANTASIES OF MEN AND WOMEN

QUESTION
What about *sexual* fantasies?

The other afternoon, a group of us who share a sailboat got together to take in our pier for the winter. We were sitting around, warming up with hot tea, when a woman friend began talking about her problems with men. "Even the most liberated of men," she complained, "seem to have trouble talking about their feelings. I always tell men I love *them*. Why can't they express their feelings for me?" A murmur of agreement went through the group. A middle-aged and very conservative woman observed that whoever wrote "As The World Turns" knew what women longed for. There men took *weeks* to describe their feelings.

A second woman asked, "What about men? What do they long for? Where are their fantasies played out?" One man quickly replied, "X-rated movies!"

After the laughter died down, the man explained what he meant. "Every male who grew up in the repressive fifties," he said, "grew up believing that men are sex maniacs and that women don't really like sex." Although he knew that things had changed ... that women now frankly admit they like sex ... he still had a hard time believing it. The old notions were too deeply ingrained.

His uncertainty about women sounded like a Woody Allen scenario: In *Love and Death,* Woody and Diane Keaton are shown in bed on their wedding night. He timidly starts to caress her shoulder; she jerks away. "Please," she says irritably, "not here." In *Play It Again, Sam,* a luscious countess confides to Woody that she is a nymphomaniac—she is insatiable sexually. Of course, when Woody Allen tries to kiss her, she's shocked: "What kind of a woman do you think I am?"

The men in our group agreed that, given their background, it wasn't at all surprising that their fantasies centered around women who longed for sex, begged for it, were insatiable.

Out of this discussion, two questions emerged. Interestingly enough, both have been posed by some of the men and women who have written to us. The first follows.

------·◆◆◆·------

QUESTION
Are men and women equally turned on
by their sexual fantasies?

------·◆◆◆·------

Men and women used to take it for granted that, although men often had sexual fantasies and enjoyed them, women rarely did. Men knew that when *they* sat staring into space, bits and snatches of sexy conversations, mock seduction scenes, and vivid sexual images often flashed across their minds. And they knew how exciting erotica was—most had hidden "girlie" magazines under their mattresses as teenagers and had sheepishly devoured X-rated books and movies. But it was hard for them, in fact nearly impossible for them, to believe that women were equally preoccupied with sex.

For a time, scientists supported the assumption that men's and women's fantasy lives were very different. An example: In the late 1940s and 1950s, Alfred Kinsey and his associates interviewed 16,000 American men and women about their sexual experiences. Kinsey concluded that men and women were strikingly different in their responsiveness to fantasy.

Kinsey assumed that such male/female differences were innate. He spent an entire chapter in *Sexual Behavior in the Human Female* trying to track down the neural mechanism that could account for these differences. What part of the cerebrum was important? The frontal lobes? The occipital lobes? The parietal lobes? The temporal lobes? What part did the hypothalamus play? (He concluded that all of these structures were important.)

Recently, some cracks in this fine scientific superstructure have begun to appear. Women are beginning to speak up. In *My Secret Garden,* Nancy Friday recalls how stunned her lover was when he discovered that, while she was "supposed" to be making love to him, she'd been thinking about another man.

> "Tell me what you are thinking about," the man I was actually fucking said, his words as charged as the action in my mind. As I'd never stopped to think before doing anything to him in bed (we were that sure of our spontaneity and response), I didn't stop to edit my thoughts. I told him what I'd been thinking. He got out of bed, put on his pants and went home.[5]

However, the most devastating blow to the notion that men's and women's fantasy lives are so very different has come from recent survey and laboratory research. In summarizing a host of surveys that have been run since Kinsey's time, Morton Hunt concludes that, when you ask men and women if they have sexual fantasies (and if they enjoy them) and if they get turned on by erotic books and movies, men are only *slightly* more likely than women to admit that they have, and enjoy, sexual and erotic fantasies.[6]

Further, in the last five years, scientists have begun not just to *ask* men and women how they feel about erotica, but to *measure* their arousal. Several European researchers have asked men and women to watch erotic movies—movies of men and women masturbating, petting, and having sexual relations. After the movies, they ask their subjects, "How much did these movies arouse you?" As might be expected, when you ask men and women about their reactions, the traditional male/female differences appear: men admit to being slightly more aroused.

However, it is also possible to measure sexual arousal. An aroused man gives himself away by his hardening erection (and you can measure that with a penile plethysmograph—a device that measures changes in the penis's circumference). When a woman becomes aroused, she experiences genital sensations (warmth, itching, pulsations) and vaginal moistening (and you can measure that via the vaginal plethysmograph—a device inserted in the vagina to measure changes in blood supply and moisture). When you measure how aroused the men and women are—either by asking them specific questions about their genital sensations or by measuring them—male/female differences virtually disappear.[7] Thus, the best evidence seems to suggest that men and women are both turned on by sexual fantasies.

QUESTION
Are there any differences in the kinds
of things men and women daydream about?

In the early 1970s, the Playboy Foundation hired the Research Guild to see whether Americans have changed since Kinsey's day. The Guild interviewed 2,000 men and women in 24 states. "What," the interviewers asked, "do you fantasize about when you're masturbating?" Men and women found very different kinds of things to be exciting. Here is a list of the kinds of fantasies men and women sometimes employ during masturbation.

Type of fantasy	Men	Women
Imagine that I am having intercourse with someone I love.	75%	80%
Having intercourse with strangers.	47	21
Sex with more than one person of the opposite sex at a time.	33	18
Forcing someone to have sex.	13	3
Being forced to have sex.	10	19
Having sex with someone of the same sex.	7	11

What about your own sexual fantasies? Take a moment now to consider the kinds of fantasies you have had.

In summarizing this and other fantasy studies, two authors note: "Male sexual fantasies are likely to involve the male in a situation where he is powerful and aggressive in getting sex in a relatively impersonal encounter. . . . In contrast, female fantasies are either highly romantic . . . or involve a woman being forced to submit in a sexual situation." They go on to say, however, that the *point* of these seemingly radically different male/female fantasies is exactly the same.

> Both males and females are aroused by fantasies of themselves as worthy; males establish their worth by imagining themselves as powerful and aggressive, while females establish their worth by imagining themselves as highly valuable either as love objects or sex objects. The content of male and female sexual fantasies in our culture is apparently highly influenced by cultural stereotypes of appropriate masculine and feminine behavior.[9]

Men's and women's fantasies have the same goal: both men and women long to be loved and desired. They also seem to want to shrug off responsibility for doing the forbidden: "It wasn't my fault; she was begging for it." "It wasn't my fault; he made me." It is only the way in which their desires are played out that differs.

LOVE: THE REALITY

Love need not be based solely on fantasy. Sometimes our fantasies come true. Now and then we encounter a person who promises to satisfy our long-unfulfilled needs—and does. When this happens, we are likely to respond joyously, and this joy itself may fuel our passion.

It all sounds simple enough, until we remember a fundamental human paradox that affects us all. We all need security, the comfort of someone who understands us, who cares for us, and who we know will be around, through thick and thin, until we're old. At the same time, we all long for excitement, novelty, and danger. We're torn between our need for one and our longing for the other.

———— ⚬◡◡◡⚬ ————

(*Terrified*) "You don't need me, do you?"
"No."
(*Equally terrified*) "You won't leave me, will you?"
"No."

———— ⚬◡◡◡⚬ ————

THE DESIRE FOR SECURITY

Men and women need security desperately. Developmental psychologists once believed in the "cupboard theory" of infant love: they thought that infants became attached to their mothers because they received milk from them. The pioneer observations of Harry and Margaret Harlow showed that these psychologists were wrong. Food is important—but what's really important for the development of love is that the mother be soft, warm, and rocking; someone to cling to, especially when you're uncertain about the world. Even a bogus "mother" made of wire and cloth will do. If she's clingable, she's lovable.

The yearning to be understood

We all need someone who understands us—someone to share our triumphs and to be around when things go desperately wrong. A few of our cor-

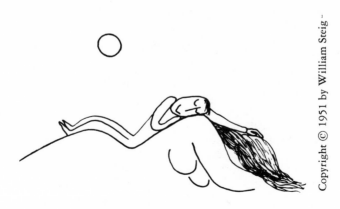

Copyright © 1951 by William Steig

We were so right together.

respondents have expressed eloquently how it feels to be a stranger, the oddball who fits in nowhere ... and then to meet someone who understands.

> Previously, in all the relationships I've had with women, it has always seemed as though all they wanted was to do things like go out to expensive places so they could talk about it with their girlfriends. I never had the feeling that they were interested in understanding me. True, I don't have very conventional interests (I like jazz—Bix Beiderbicke and Louis Armstrong and Model A's—not rock music and hot rods). Maybe that's part of why I think it's so great that I finally found a girl who really cares about what I think—my likes and dislikes. She would just as soon sit around and talk as go out to some fancy restaurant and a show.
>
> An 18-year-old logger from Alaska

> I can't believe how much we are on the same vibes. He just called and after a lengthy conversation, and after reading the letter I got from him today, I realized that we have been thinking the same thing!
>
> I realize I just might have met my husband. And I think he's having similar thoughts. All I do is think about him, and I can't even remember exactly what he looks like!! This is ridiculous. I'm usually calm and cool and collected.
>
> A waitress in Wisconsin

Actor Robert Redford fell in love with Lola Von Wagenen because she understood him.

> Before I met Lola, I traveled. It was a great education in a lot of ways, but I felt a terrible low in Italy. I was completely alone and I felt like I'd aged and become an old man. No one I knew could relate to the feeling of isolation I had and I started drinking worse than ever. After Italy I went back in 1957 to California—that's where I come from. Lola was just out of high school and her attitude was so fresh and responsive. I had so much to say to her, that I started talking, sometimes all night long. She was genuinely interested in what I had to say, at a time when I really needed to talk.
>
> There were nights when we would walk around Hollywood Hills and start talking, like after dinner; walk down Hollywood Boulevard to Sunset, then up Sunset to the top of the hills, then over to the Hollywood Bowl and back to watch the dawn come up—and we'd still be talking. I had always said I'd never get married before I was 35, but my instincts told me that this was a person I'd like to go through life with.[10]

The yearning to have someone take care of us

Simple understanding is wonderful. But now and then, we get even more. Someone recognizes our need and responds to it. Someone saves us. Such "rescues" are the stuff of romantic novels.

In the eighteenth and nineteenth centuries, melodrama thrived. A typical playbill introduced theatergoers to such characters as "Jenny: a gentle country girl," saved from the clutches of "The Squire: cruel and licentious," "Jarvis Quaffcup: his bumbling servant," and "Timothy Thorowgood, who, at the last second, and after a series of amazing coincidences, is able to pluck Jenny from a fate worse than death."

In the early twentieth century, melodrama moved to the screen. In *The Perils of Pauline,* Pauline was rescued again and again from the edges of cliffs, the ledges of buildings, and onrushing trains. Sometimes, the hero got rescued; sometimes, they kept each other company while waiting to be saved.

This theme—of a lover who cares for his beloved in the most impossible of circumstances—is a timeless one. It continues to be popular today.

"Rescues" are often the stuff of romantic movies and novels. (Photo courtesy of Wisconsin Center for Film and Theater Research.)

For example, the English romantic novelist, Barbara Cartland, has written more than 150 best-selling romantic novels. What does she write about? Consider this excerpt from *Love and the Loathsome Leopard:*

> Wivina gave a cry of horror and put out her hands to ward him off. He caught her in his arms and, while she struggled frantically, she realised that he was very strong and she was completely helpless.
>
> ... "I'll bed you now!" he said roughly. "And that'll settle the matter once and for all!"
>
> Struggling and fighting against him, Wivina felt herself pulled across the room.
>
> ... She was half-sprawling on the floor, and picking her up in his arms, he flung her down on the bed. Then, as she screamed in sheer terror, there was a sudden bright explosion which shook the whole house. It seemed to be followed by complete silence. Then shouts and screams broke out, to be followed by yet another explosion—the vibrating boom of a ship's gun.

(It was the Lord Cheriton—the "Loathsome Leopard"—who had commandeered the *H.M.S. Valiant* to save her.)

> She met him at the top of the stairs and he pulled her close to him. As he did so, she burst into tears.
>
> "Oh, Leopard ... Leopard!" she sobbed. "I prayed that you would ... save me. ..."
>
> "You are safe, my darling," he answered. .... He put his fingers under her chin and turned her face up to his.
>
> "What have you done to me?" he asked. "I have always been a soldier, thinking only of battles, of fighting, of victories. Now all I want to be is a country squire sitting by my fireside with my wife and my dogs, planning the rotation of crops."[11]

At one time or another, we all long for security. When we meet someone who is able to buffer us from life's frustrations and tribulations, we're bound to feel immense relief and the pleasure we feel can add a glow to our passionate feelings. But once we become really secure, we stop focusing on what we have—security—and start longing for what we don't have—excitement. Here is psychoanalyst John Bowlby's description of the way the desire for security and the desire for freedom alternate in the small child:

> James Anderson describes watching two-year-olds whilst their mothers sit quietly on a seat in a London park. Slipping free from the mother, a two-year-old would typically move away from her in short bursts punc-

*On the other hand, once we become really
secure, we stop focusing on what we have
—security—and start longing for what we
don't have—excitement.*

tuated by halts. Then, after a more prolonged halt, he would return to
her—usually in faster and longer bursts. Once returned, however, he
would proceed again on another foray, only to return once more. It was
as though he were tied to his mother by some invisible elastic that
stretches so far and then brings him back to base.[12]

In his research, Bowlby has found that when a child's mother is
around, he's not very interested in her. He looks at her, sees that everything is okay, and sallies forth. Now and then he sneaks a quick glance to
make sure she's still there or to find out whether she still approves of what
he's doing, but then he's off again. Should his mother disappear for a
moment, it's a different story. The child becomes very depressed—or very
distressed and agitated. He devotes all his energy to searching for her. New
adventures lose all allure. Of course, once she returns, he's off again.

Sound familiar? Obviously the child remains in all of us. Often, it's
when we're most secure in our loving relationships that we find our minds
wandering to castles—and lovers—in Spain.

THE DESIRE FOR EXCITEMENT

The sixteenth-century author John Lyly sagely commented that "danger and delight grow on one stalk." Anyone who has climbed aboard a roller-coaster or launched a hang glider can testify to the truth of his statement. Most of us possess a restless desire for excitement. As one psychologist observed:

> A superficial examination of Western man reveals a creature of great discontent. He spends a great amount of time in the "pursuit of happiness," but reaching the goals which define "happiness" rarely ends the pursuit. Instead, goals are redefined and the pursuit continues. It seems that the pursuit is more essential than the goal. The restless drive of humankind to seek out the novel, to explore the limits of mind, muscles, and senses, to take great risks in spite of fear, to release the animal brain from the constraints of the social brain, may be the source of both his creativeness and his destructiveness.[13]

Although scientists aren't quite sure *why* people crave excitement, two explanations seem especially popular: first, it feels good to have **variety** in your life—lack of variety is actually painful; second, any animal must

Courtesy of RKO General Pictures.

Some people need far more excitement than do others.

maintain an optimal level of stimulation in order to be alert, to function, and to develop.

Other scientists offer still different explanations as to why people sometimes actually seek out emotional turmoil, trouble, and danger. Whatever their theory, all psychologists agree on one thing: people *need* excitement.

Some people need far more excitement than do others. Further, people need more excitement at certain times than they do at other times. To measure such person-to-person and day-to-day variations, psychologist Marvin Zuckerman developed the "Sensation Seeking Scale" (the SSS). A few of the items that Zuckerman and his colleagues developed to measure *excitement* follow. How many of the exciting alternatives would you agree with? (They are marked with an asterisk.)

THE SENSATION SEEKING SCALE (SSS) [14]

1. *_____ I would like a job which would require a lot of traveling.

    _____ I would prefer a job in one location.

2. *_____ I am invigorated by a brisk, cold day.

    _____ I can't wait to get indoors on a cold day.

3. _____ I dislike all body odors.

    *_____ I like some of the earthy body smells.

4. _____ I would not like to try any drug which might produce strange and dangerous effects on me.

    *_____ I would like to try some of the new drugs that produce hallucinations.

5. _____ I would prefer living in an ideal society where everyone is safe, secure, and happy.

    *_____ I would have preferred living in the unsettled days of our history.

6. _____ I can't stand riding with a person who likes to speed.

    *_____ I sometimes like to drive very fast because I find it exciting.

7. _____ If I were a salesman, I would prefer a straight salary, rather than the risk of making little or nothing on a commission basis.

   *_____ If I were a salesman, I would prefer working on a commission if I had a chance to make more money than I could on salary.

8. _____ I don't like to argue with people whose beliefs are sharply divergent from mine, since such arguments are never resolved.

   *_____ I find people who disagree with my beliefs more stimulating than people who agree with me.

9. *_____ Most people spend entirely too much money on life insurance.

   _____ Life insurance is something that no person can afford to be without.

10. _____ I would not like to be hypnotized.

    *_____ I would like to have the experience of being hypnotized.

11. *_____ The most important goal of life is to live it to the fullest and experience as much of it as you can.

    _____ The most important goal of life is to find peace and happiness.

12. _____ I enter cold water gradually giving myself time to get used to it.

    *_____ I like to dive or jump right into the ocean or a cold pool.

13. _____ I do not like the irregularity and discord of most modern music.

    *_____ I like to listen to new and unusual kinds of music.

14. _____ The worst social sin is to be rude.

    *_____ The worst social sin is to be a bore.

15. *_____ I prefer people who are emotionally expressive even if they are a bit unstable.

_____ I prefer people who are calm and even tempered.

16. _____ People who ride motorcycles must have some kind of an unconscious need to hurt themselves.

*_____ I would like to drive or ride on a motorcycle.

When you're eager for excitement, there are a variety of ways to stir it up. We've mentioned several—but there's still another. You can get involved in exciting, passionate relationships. Zuckerman has found that high-stimulation seekers often do find romantic confrontations an appealing way to generate a little excitement. For example, in one study, he asked people to fill out the SSS. Then he asked them to tell him (anonymously) a little bit about their sexual behavior. He posed such questions as: Have you ever kissed another person? Petted? Had intercourse? How? With the man on top? The woman on top? Side to side? Have you ever engaged in fellatio? Cunnilingus? Zuckerman found a fairly substantial relationship between people's SSS scores and their sexual experience.

Passion and excitement are tightly—and perhaps inextricably—linked. When you're in love, it's exciting; when you experience the delight of really getting to know someone or of exploring a new sexual relationship, it's exciting. Your excitement intensifies your passion and it's easy to conclude that you're in love; the two kindle and rekindle one another.

Two aspects of love relations are particularly exciting and are particularly likely to ignite passion—the excitement of getting to know someone and the excitement of sex.

The excitement of getting to know someone

A new relationship is exciting. It's exciting to see if you'll be attractive to someone. It's exciting to explore another person's personality, to find out what he or she _really_ thinks about things. It's exciting to try things you would never think of trying. One of the delights in life is getting to know another person well. As two of our correspondents observed:

One of the most terrifying _and_ exciting things about having an illicit affair is that I'm never quite sure if he'll think I'm attractive. I'm terrified that he'll be shocked when he sees me undressed. I'm starting to get old. I'm starting to have some grey hair, some wrinkles, my breasts are beginning to sag. I'm getting crêpey thighs. I worry that he'll be turned off . . . repulsed. When he says that I'm beautiful, I'm relieved and excited. I feel like I've been granted a little more time in life.

One thing that I'm trying to do in this affair is to be totally honest. I've never been brave enough to try that before. I tell myself that since we don't know each other, that it's really not *too* dangerous—I really don't have anything to lose. So, I've tried saying, honestly, how I feel about things. He's responded in kind. Paradoxically, that's made things so good . . . that I'm more nervous now than ever. Now I *am* starting to have something to lose.

The wife of an Army sergeant in
Texarkana, Texas

The reason that I have always been fascinated by my husband is that I can never predict what he'll be thinking. Sometimes when we're lying in bed at night and he's looking sort of bemused, I'll bend over and say, "What are you thinking about, honey?" Of course, I expect that he'll be thinking that he loves me, or My God, thinking about some other woman . . . or something like that. He never is. He'll say something like, "I'm thinking about how you could go about constructing a giant clock—one that had all the planets in the right position and they'd all rotate around one another at just the right times. I was wondering how big it would have to be to have everything in the right position."

It sounds like a peculiar basis for love, but I think that the thing I love best about him is the way his mind works . . . and that's more than enough.

A teacher from Detroit

And then there's sex.

The excitement of sex

The poet e e cummings expressed well the unique excitement of love-making:

> i like my body when it is with your
> body. It is so quite new a thing.
> Muscles better and nerves more.
> i like your body. i like what it does,
> i like its hows. i like to feel the spine
> of your body and its bones, and the trembling
> -firm-smooth ness and which i will
> again and again and again
> kiss, i like kissing this and that of you,
> i like, slowly stroking the, shocking fuzz
> of your electric fur, and what-is-it comes
> over parting flesh . . . . And eyes big love-crumbs,
>
> and possibly i like the thrill
>
> of under me you so quite new.[15]

Sex is always exciting. When we're caught up in a sexual encounter, our faces flush, our hearts pound, and we become very aroused. (Or, in Masters and Johnson's terms: "Sexual intercourse induces hyperventilation, tachycardia, and marked increases in blood pressure.") Sex is probably most exciting when there's some novelty in the form of lovemaking, in the site of lovemaking, or in our partner.

The Coolidge Effect. Biologists have observed that, in lower animals, males' sexual responsiveness is fueled by just the right combination of familiarity and novelty. On one hand, some degree of security fosters sexual arousal. For example, Kinsey reports that many animals (e.g., the monkey and the porcupine) will *only* copulate with familiar females; other animals (such as cats and dogs) become sexually excited when they approach places where they have previously had sexual experience.[16]

At the same time, animals who live together for prolonged periods often show "psychologic fatigue"—i.e., they simply lose sexual interest in each other. Researchers Frank Beach and Lisbeth Jordan allowed male and female rats to copulate until they were "exhausted"—or rather, until the *males* were exhausted; female rats can go on forever. Beach and Jordan found that it took these male rats ten to fifteen days to rest up sufficiently to resume copulation at their usual rate.[17]

Allen Fisher pointed out that, even for rats, there's a difference between "exhaustion" and "boredom." Fisher found that if immediately after the male rat reached exhaustion he replaced the original female with a new one, the exhausted male suddenly had no difficulty performing. Moreover, if the male were supplied with a new partner after that—and still another partner after that—he managed to double or even triple the number of ejaculations he had before again becoming exhausted.[18]

Thus, it appears that satiated rats—just like tired husbands or wives—can be aroused by a novel partner. This phenomenon has been labeled, somewhat whimsically, the "Coolidge Effect," after an anecdote concerning President Coolidge. It seems that, during a visit to a large chicken farm, the president fell somewhat behind his wife. As the story goes: "Mrs. Coolidge, observing the vigor with which one particularly prominent rooster covered hen after hen, asked the guide to make certain that the President took note of the rooster's behavior. When President Coolidge got to the hen yard, the rooster was pointed out and his exploits recounted by the guide, who added that Mrs. Coolidge had requested that the President be made aware of the rooster's prowess. The President reflected for a moment and replied, 'Tell Mrs. Coolidge that there is more than one hen.' "[19]

How we respond to the new man or woman we meet at a party, at work, or in our neighborhood depends in part on how appealing that person would normally be to us, as well as on how sexually turned-on (or turned-off) we happen to be at the time we meet.

In one study, researchers invited men and women to view some slides. One group was asked to rate nineteen erotic slides. The slides showed young men and women in almost every combination, position, and sexual activity imaginable. Needless to say, both men and women reported that these slides were very arousing. Other men and women were shown geometric figures—a definite turn-off. They rated the slides . . . and that was presumably that. Both groups left to participate in a second (supposedly unrelated) project.

When they arrived at their second appointment, each was introduced to a work partner—a college man or woman. Since their partners were already busily engaged in filling out questionnaires, they all quickly got down to work. The experimenter filmed the session.

The researchers found that men and women in a highly aroused state reacted very differently to their new acquaintances than did those in a "nothing special" state. When aroused men and women were working with someone of the opposite sex, they behaved a lot more erotically than usual. (For example, they gazed at their partners more frequently than they normally would.) When men and women were working with someone of the same sex, however, men gazed at men less often than usual. (Apparently, they felt uncomfortable talking to another man while feeling twinges of sexual arousal. They seemed to go out of their way to say, "Not me.") Women weren't so nervous; if anything, women were slightly more likely to gaze at women when they were experiencing the after-twinges of sexual arousal.[20]

TRYING TO RECONCILE THE UNRECONCILABLE

It appears, then, that both the man or woman who offers us security *and* the man or woman who threatens to shatter our snug, cozy existence can stimulate a strong passionate response.

QUESTION

Should I tell the person I love
that I love him/her (security)?
Or should I play hard to get
(excitement)?

According to folklore, a woman who "throws herself" at another inspires less passion than does a person who is hard to get. The *Kama Sutra of*

Vatsyayana advises women to use the following strategy to "gain over a man."

> But old authors say that although the girl loves the man ever so much she should not offer herself or make the first overtures, for a girl who does this loses her dignity, and is liable to be scorned and rejected. But when the man tries to kiss her she should oppose him; when he begs to be allowed to have sexual intercourse with her she should let him touch her private parts only and with considerable difficulty; and though importuned by him, she should not yield herself up to him as if of her own accord, but should resist his attempts to have her. It is only, moreover, when she is certain that she is truly loved, and that her lover is indeed devoted to her, and will not change his mind, that she should then give herself up to him, and persuade him to marry her quickly. After losing her virginity she should tell her confidential friends about it.
>
> Here end the efforts of a girl to gain over a man.[21]

Socrates, Ovid, the *Kama Sutra,* Bertrand Russell, and "Dear Abby" all agree: love is stimulated by excitement and challenge. To find authors in such rare accord is refreshing. Unfortunately (but fortunately for the rest of us), it looks as if the sages were wrong. In the early 1970s, when we first began our investigations, we assumed that the sages were right. We accepted cultural lore.

We began our research with men. We began not by asking men *if* they preferred an easy-to-get or a hard-to-get girl, but by asking them *why* they disdained easy-to-get women and desired hard-to-get ones. Most men were cooperative. They explained that an easy-to-get woman spells trouble. (She is probably desperate for a date. She is probably the kind of woman who makes too many demands on a person, the kind who wants to get serious right away. Even worse, she might have a "disease.")

The elusive woman, on the other hand, is almost inevitably a valuable woman. The men pointed out that a woman can only afford to be choosy if she is popular—and a woman is popular for some reason. When a woman is hard to get, it's usually a tip-off that she is especially pretty, has a good personality, is sexy, and so on. Men also were intrigued by the challenge that the elusive woman offers; one can spend a great deal of time fantasizing about what it would be like to date her. Also, since the hard-to-get woman's desirability is well recognized, a man can gain prestige if he is seen with her. In brief, nearly all men took it for granted (as we did) that men prefer hard-to-get women and they could supply abundant justification for their prejudice.

A few isolated men refused to cooperate. These dissenters noted that an elusive woman is not always more desirable than an available woman.

Sometimes the hard-to-get woman is not only hard to get—she is impossible to get, because she is misanthropic and cold. Sometimes a woman is easy to get simply because she is a friendly, outgoing person who boosts one's ego and ensures that dates are "no hassle." We ignored the testimony of these deviant types.

We then conducted five experiments designed to demonstrate that an individual values a hard-to-get date more highly than an easy-to-get date. All five experiments failed. Let's consider one of these disasters.

A flurry of advertisements appeared on campus inviting college men and women to sign up for a free computer-date-matching service. In an initial interview, men and women told the computer all about themselves.

Two weeks later, the "dating bureau" asked the men to drop by to collect the name and telephone number of their date-matches. The dating counselor also asked them for a favor. Would they telephone their date from the office, invite her out, and then report on their first impression of her? (Presumably, the counselor was interested in how the matches seemed to be working out.)

In fact, the dating bureau had been very busy during the two-week lull. They had contacted the women who had signed up for the computer matching program and hired them as experimenters. They had given the women precise instructions on how they should act when their computer matches called them for a date. Half of the women were told to play hard to get. When a man asked them out, they were to pause . . . and think . . . and think . . . for three or four seconds before replying: "Mm (*slight pause*). No, I've got a date then. It seems like I signed up for that date match thing a long time ago and I've met more people since then—I'm really pretty busy all this week." When the man suggested another time, they were to accept reluctantly.

Half of the women were told to act easy to get. They were to eagerly accept the man's offer of a coffee date.

All five experiments we conducted had the same results: men liked the easy-to-get women and the hard-to-get women equally well.[22] So, if you're interested in attracting someone, playing hard to get isn't necessarily the answer.

How, then, should we behave? Should we admit to others that we love them (thus offering them security)? Or should we play hard to get? The best answer seems to be: Act naturally. It's impossible to predict what others will like: some people are attracted to the candid, friendly type; others prefer those who are coolly aloof. There's nothing to be gained from *playing* at one role or another, so you might as well speak frankly and act freely. Express your admiration for those you like, your hopes for the relationship—and any doubts you have about either one.

five
The pain of passionate love

*It seems that sexual desire can easily blend with and be stimulated
by any strong emotion, of which love is only one. . . .
Sexual desire can be stimulated by the anxiety of aloneness,
by the wish to conquer or be conqured, by vanity, by the wish to hurt
and even to destroy, as much as it can be stimulated by love.*

Erich Fromm
The Art of Loving

QUESTION

This love affair is so frustrating. Why am
I subjecting myself to all this misery?

ANSWER

Maybe you love someone not *in spite* of
the frustration and anxiety they cause you,
but *because* of it.

From infancy on, it's not uncommon for us to react to an unsettling event with a sexual response. When baby boys are emotionally upset —restless, fretting, crying—they almost always have an erection.[1] Adolescents often associate anxiety with sexuality. When preadolescent boys were asked if they ever found themselves responding erotically in a nonsexual situation, they mentioned "accidents or near accidents," "being late to school," "playing in exciting games," "report cards," "fast car driving," "being angry at another boy," and "looking over the edge of a building" as arousing experiences.[2] Girls report similar feelings.

Adults are also peculiarly susceptible to love and sex during times of emotional upheaval. In his autobiography, Bertrand Russell reports that an irrelevant, frightening event—World War I—intensified his passion for Colette, a mistress:

> We scarcely knew each other, and yet in that moment there began for both of us a relation profoundly serious and profoundly important, sometimes happy, sometimes painful, but never unworthy to be placed alongside of the great public emotions connected with the War. Indeed, the War was bound into the texture of this love from first to last. The first time that I was ever in bed with her (we did not go to bed the first time we were lovers, as there was too much to say), we heard suddenly a shout of bestial triumph in the street. I leapt out of bed and saw a zeppelin falling in flames. The thought of brave men dying in agony was what caused the triumph in the street. Collette's love was in that moment a refuge to me.[3]

Romantic passion is often enhanced by unpleasant but arousing states, such as anxiety and fear, frustration, jealousy, loneliness, and anger.

ANXIETY AND FEAR

Some lovers seem to experience more anxiety than joy when they encounter their beloved face to face. Consider salesman Jim Reynold:

80

I met Helen about a year ago, at a company party. About four times a year the company calls in the regional sales directors, suggests what we might do to improve sales—and then soothes everyone's bruised egos by finishing up with a wild party.

For me these meetings are an excruciating—and delicious—mixture of hope and anxiety. A week or so before the party, I'm in a fever. I think about the witty things I'll say to Helen, the warm conversations we'll have, and think how exciting it will be to invite her up to my apartment; I think about how wonderful it will be to make love to her.

Immediately before the party, everything changes. I'm terrified. I'm so nervous I start to perspire; sweat beads up on my upper lip, makes rings on my shirt. Once I get there and actually see her, it's even worse. I want so much to make a good impression that I'm incapacitated. I'm afraid to do anything.

Anxiety is not merely an unpleasant side effect of love; rather, it actually helps foster passion. A group of Canadian physiologists conducted an

From earliest infancy on, men and women often respond to an unsettling event with a sexual response.

interesting experiment to determine the connection between anxiety and sexual arousal. The researchers asked women to view three different video films:

- *Anxiety film:* This film depicted, in vivid detail, several horrifying automobile accidents. In some instances, the occupant's death cries could be heard.
- *Neutral film:* A travelogue about Nova Scotia.
- *Sexual film:* This erotic film showed a nude couple engaging in foreplay; they stopped just at the point of intercourse.

After the women were caught up in one of the three films, another film flashed on. How did women respond when they viewed: The erotic and then the horrifying film? The erotic and then the neutral film? The horrifying and then the erotic film? The neutral and then the erotic film? If the grotesquely horrible movie flashed on just as the women were beginning to feel pleasantly aroused by the sexy movie, the women became more anxious (although not significantly so) and far less aroused than usual. However, if the accident film preceded the sexy movie, something peculiar happened: the anxious women became far *more* aroused than they would normally be. Somehow, anxiety intensified rather than extinguished their sexual feelings.[4] Apparently, a certain amount of anxiety or tension actually heightens our sexual response. There is evidence, then, that under the right conditions, passion can be ignited by anxiety.

What about fear? Two psychologists discovered a close link between fear and sexual attraction. In one experiment, the researchers invited men and women to participate in a learning experiment. When the men showed up, they discovered that their "partner" was a strikingly beautiful woman. They also discovered that, by signing up for the experiment, they'd gotten into more than they'd bargained for. The experimenter was studying the effects of electric shock on learning. Sometimes the experimenter quickly went on to reassure the men that they'd been assigned to a control group and would be receiving only a barely perceptible "tingle" of a shock. Other times, the experimenter tried to terrify the men: he warned them that they'd be getting some pretty painful electrical shocks.

Before the supposed experiment was to begin, the experimenter approached each man privately and asked how he felt about the beautiful coed who "happened" to be his partner. He asked the man to tell him—in confidence—how attracted he was to her (e.g., "How much would you like to ask her out for a date?" "How much would you like to kiss her?"). The investigators predicted—as any good social psychologist would—that fear would facilitate attraction. And it did. The terrified men found the women a lot sexier than did the calm and cool men.[5]

In another study, the psychologists compared reactions of young men crossing two bridges in North Vancouver. The first, Capilano Canyon Suspension Bridge, is a 450-foot-long, five-foot-wide span that tilts, sways, and wobbles over a 230-foot drop to rocks and shallow rapids below. The other bridge, a bit farther upstream, is a solid, safe structure.

As each young man crossed the bridge, a good-looking college student approached him. She explained that she was doing a class project and asked if he would fill out a questionnaire for her. When the man had finished, the woman offered to explain her project in greater detail "when I have more time." She wrote her telephone number on a small piece of paper so that the man could call her if he wanted more information. Which men called? Why the men who met the coed under frightening conditions, of course. (Nine of the thirty-three men on the suspension bridge called her. Only two of the men on the solid bridge called.)[6]

So, strange as it sounds, adrenalin makes the heart grow fonder. Anxiety and fear, unpleasant as they may be, can play a large part in fueling passionate love.

FRUSTRATION

Khrushchev, depicting the Russian character, once said: "When the aristocrats first discovered potatoes were a cheap way of feeding the peasants, they had no success in getting the peasants to eat them. But they knew their people. They fenced the potatoes in with high fences. The peasants then stole the potatoes and soon acquired a taste for them."[7]

Although it is not clear that "absence makes the heart grow fonder," there is evidence that the obstacles lovers encounter in pursuit of their beloved often intensify love. The passion of wartime romances, unrequited loves, and extramarital affairs is fueled—in part, anyway—by frustration.

Freud claims that our romantic feelings begin with the arousal associated with *inhibited* sexuality: "Some obstacle is necessary to swell the tide of libido to its height; and at all periods of history whenever natural barriers in the way of satisfaction have not sufficed, mankind has erected conventional ones in order to enjoy love."[8]

Writers of erotica understand Freud's principle perfectly. Ultimately, sex means a lot more if, when you're sexually excited, your partner teases you a little to heighten your desire for sex before satisfying it.

In 1940, a collector of erotica offered *Tropic of Cancer* author Henry Miller a hundred dollars a month to write erotic stories. He passed up the 'offer, but suggested that his friend Anaïs Nin might be interested. She was. Nin and several friends invented fantasies, quizzed the people they met about their fantasies, researched them via Krafft-Ebing and medical books, and described their own.

The following excerpt from one of their sexiest stories illustrates Freud's theme: the intensification of sexual arousal via frustration—and finally, fulfillment.

He began by slowly tearing her dress from around her belt. Louise was trembling at the strength of his hands. She stood naked now except for the heavy silver belt. He loosened her hair over her shoulders. And only then did he bend her back on the bed and kiss her interminably, his hands over her breasts. Her sexual hunger was rising like madness to her head, blinding her. It was so urgent that she could not wait. She could not even wait until he undressed. But Antonio ignored her movements of impatience. She was moist and trembling, opening her legs and trying to climb over him. She tried to open his pants.

"There is time," he said. "There is plenty of time. We are going to stay in this room for days. There is a lot of time for both of us."

She was trying to satisfy her hunger by rubbing against his leg, but he would not let her. He bent her as if she were made of rubber, twisted her into every position. With his two strong hands he took whatever part of her he was hungry for and brought it up to his mouth like a morsel of food, not caring how the rest of her body fell into space.

By this time the hunger in her womb was like a raging fire. She thought that it would drive her insane. Whatever she tried to do to bring herself to an orgasm, he defeated. If she even kissed him too long he would break away.

They were both panting and twisting, and only then did he lift her up, carry her to the bed, and put her legs around his shoulders. He took her violently and they shook and trembled as they came together. She fell away suddenly and sobbed hysterically. The orgasm had been so strong that she had thought she would go insane, with a hatred and a joy like nothing she had ever known. He was smiling, panting; they lay back and fell asleep.[9]

Judging by Louise's experience, sexual deprivation seems to be at least as arousing as sexual gratification. Actually, *anything* connected with sex seems to be arousing!

------------◦◦◦------------
QUESTION
What is the best way for parents
to break up a relationship?
ANSWER
Mind their own business.
------------◦◦◦------------

Many parents have short memories: they forget just how they felt when their own parents tried to interfere in their affairs; how adamant they became about continuing a forbidden love relationship. So, frequently, they repeat the mistake with their own offspring. More often than not, parental interference seems to intensify romantic feelings rather than dampening them. Consider this young woman's description of how she got involved in a disastrous marriage:

> I really had no idea what marriage was like. I had no idea at all, and jumped into it like we were playing a game—playing house. And, oh, another big factor I forgot to mention. Because he was divorced, my mother automatically labeled him unfit, and this was a big factor in pushing me to him. She liked him when she met him, she liked the kind of work he did, she liked his age, his appearance, all of those things, but as soon as she heard he was divorced, he was suddenly rotten, no good, bad, unfit, and it really rankled me. And marrying him was another means of defiance. By God, I was going to do this thing—and did, to my sorrow.[10]

Romeo and Juliet, Johnse Hatfield and Rose Anne McCoy, Abelard and Eloise—all these famous, and very passionate, lovers shared one common problem: their families were bitter enemies. Apparently, an affair consummated without major difficulty lacks zest.

One psychologist found support for his contention that parental opposition deepens romantic love. He and fellow researchers invited thirty-one dating couples (eighteen of the thirty-one couples were living together) and ninety-one married couples to participate in a marital-relations project. The interviewer quizzed couples separately about two things:

- *Parental interference:* To what extent do your parents interfere in your relationship and cause trouble? Have your parents become more—or less—interfering lately?
- *Romantic love scale:* How romantically do you feel about your partner—both in general and lately?

The researchers found compelling evidence that their supposition was correct. As soon as their parents became resigned to a relationship and began to interfere less, the lovers' interest in one another began to wane. When parents became concerned about a relationship and began to interfere more and more, the couples generally fell more deeply in love.[11] Thus, parental interference is likely to boomerang. It tends to foster desire rather than divisiveness.

JEALOUSY

No matter how perfect—or practically perfect—a wife may be, she always has to watch out for the Other Woman. The Other Woman, according to my definition, is anyone able to charm my husband, amuse my husband, attract my husband, or occupy his wholehearted interest for more than 30 seconds straight.

Judith Viorst, *Yes Married*

Simone de Beauvoir, in *The Woman Destroyed,* writes about a jealous wife's collapsing world. It is a painful chronicle. The woman is in her fifties. If you asked her if she loved her husband, she would say, "Of course," but the passion in their relationship has long ago flickered out. They now simply take one another for granted. She spends her days comfortably—visiting with her children, shopping, helping friends. When her husband, Maurice, admits that he is having an affair, everything changes. The wife is alternately calm and frantic. She wants to hurt and punish him; she disdains him; and she loves him more than ever.

> And I went to have a talk with Isabelle [a friend].... She advised me to be patient. What gives this sort of affair its piquancy is its newness; time works against Noellie; the glamour she may have in Maurice's eyes will fade. But if I want our love to emerge from this trial unhurt I must play neither the victim nor the shrew. "Be understanding, be cheerful. Above all be friendly," she said to me.... Patience is not my outstanding virtue. But I certainly must do my best.[12]

Moments later, her fantasies and discoveries plunge her into despair. She minutely calculates how much time Maurice spends with her versus Noellie. She calls Maurice's office to check on him and camps outside Noellie's apartment in the hopes of seeing them together, hoping she can gauge the intensity of Maurice's love for Noellie by his gaze, by how they walk together. She both avoids information and seeks it desperately.

I am afraid of sleeping, on the nights that Maurice spends with Noellie. That empty bed next to mine, these flat, cold sheets. . . . I take sleeping pills, but in vain, for I dream. Often in my dreams I faint with distress. I no longer know anything. The whole of my past life has collapsed behind me, as the land does in those earthquakes where the ground consumes and destroys itself—is swallowed up behind you as you flee. There is no going back. I am so destroyed by the morning that if the daily woman did not come at ten o'clock I should stay in bed every day until past noon, as I do on Sundays. Why doesn't he love me anymore? The question is why did he love me in the first place. One never asks oneself.[13]

Simone de Beauvoir's chronicle details the chaotic jumble of emotions that jealousy creates. What do social scientists know about these painful feelings?

THE THEORY AND RESEARCH

———————•◊◊◊•———————

QUESTION

What is jealousy anyway?

———————•◊◊◊•———————

Although jealousy is hard to describe—fifty people will give you fifty different descriptions—it's an extremely common emotion, one that almost all of us experience at some point in our lives. Most theorists agree that jealousy has two basic components: (1) a feeling of battered pride, and (2) a feeling that one's property rights have been violated.

According to such notables as Sigmund Freud, Otto Fenichel, and anthropologist Margaret Mead, jealousy is "really" little more than bruised pride. Margaret Mead, for example, observes that the more shaky one's self-esteem, the more vulnerable one is to jealousy: "Jealousy is not a barometer by which the depth of love can be read. It merely records the degree of the lover's insecurity. . . . It is a negative miserable state of feeling having its origin in the sense of insecurity and inferiority."[14]

According to others, jealousy is "really" little more than one's fear of losing one's property. In 1936, sociologist Kingsley Davis provided a fascinating sociological analysis of jealousy:

There are thus two dangers which beset any person with regard to property. The first is that somebody will win out over him in legitimate competition. This is the danger of superior rivalry. The second is that somebody will illegitimately take from him property already acquired. . . . This is the danger of trespass. . . .

*Jealousy is "really" little more than
fear of losing one's property.*

Most malignant emotions are concerned with these two dangers,
being directed either at a rival or trespasser or at someone who is helping a rival or trespasser. . . . In general fear and hatred of rivals is
institutionally suppressed; fear and hatred of trespassers encouraged.
. . . Our malignant emotions, fear, anger, hate, and jealousy, greet any
illicit attempt to gain property that we hold.[15]

QUESTION

Do men and women respond any
differently when they're jealous?

There are striking differences in the way men and women respond to jealousy: "Men are more apt to *deny* jealous feelings; women are more apt to
acknowledge them. Men are more likely than women to express jealous
feelings through rage and even violence, but such outbursts are often fol-
lowed by despondency. Jealous men are more apt to focus on the outside
sexual activity of the partner and they often demand a recital of the intimate details; jealous women are more likely to focus on the *emotional* in-

volvement between a partner and the third party. Men are more likely to *externalize* the cause of the jealousy, more likely to blame the partner, or the third party, or 'circumstances.' Women often *internalize* the cause of jealousy; they blame themselves. Similarly, a jealous man is more likely to display *competitive* behavior toward the third party, while a jealous woman is more likely to display *possessive* behavior. She clings to her partner rather than confronting the third party."[16]

California psychologist Jeff Bryson found that most of us respond to jealousy in one of two ways: (1) some people try to protect their own egos—for example, they berate their partners, beat them up, try to get even; (2) some people try to improve their floundering relationship—they try to make themselves more attractive, talk things out, etc.

Further, men and women seem to respond quite differently to provocation. In general, jealous men concentrate on shoring up their sagging self-esteem. Jealous women are more likely to do something to strengthen the relationship.[17]

Bryson speculates that perhaps these male/female differences are due to the fact that most societies are patriarchal. It is acceptable for men to initiate relationships; thus, when they're threatened, they can easily go elsewhere. Women may not have the same freedom; thus, they devote their energies to keeping the relationship from floundering.

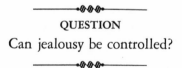

QUESTION

Can jealousy be controlled?

The answer usually depends on who you're asking.

The "traditionalists" take it for granted that marriage should be permanent and exclusive. Thus, they have a certain vested interest in believing that jealousy is a natural emotion. They generally begin their spirited defense of jealousy by pointing out that even animals are jealous. For example, Charles Darwin argued that, "Even insects express anger, terror, jealousy, and love."[18] Other naturalists—such as Ewald Bohm—vividly described the "jealous" courtship battles of stags, antelopes, wild pigs, goats, seals, kangaroos, howler monkeys, and so on.[19]

The "new humanists" see things differently. They believe that our personal lives would be more satisfying and our professional lives more creative and productive if we felt free to love all humankind—or at least a larger subset of it. Thus, they naturally prefer to believe that society has the power to arouse or to temper jealousy as it chooses.

As psychologist Ralph Hupka observes, each culture prescribes the cues that trigger jealousy. The following fictional episode, said to take place in a primitive society of approximately 100 members, better illustrates his point.

> On her return trip from the local watering well, a married woman is asked for a cup of water by a male resident of the village. Her husband, resting on the porch of their dwelling, observes his wife giving the man a cup of water. Subsequently, they approach the husband and the three of them enjoy a lively and friendly conversation into the late evening hours. Eventually the husband puts out the lamp, and the guest has sexual intercourse with the wife. The next morning the husband leaves the house early in order to catch fishes for breakfast. Upon his return he finds his wife having sex again with the guest. The husband becomes violently enraged and mortally stabs the guest.

> At what point in the vignette may one expect the husband to be jealous? It depends, of course, in which culture we place the husband. A husband of the Yurok Indian tribe of California in the 19th century challenged any man to a fight who dared to request a cup of water from his wife. An Ammassalik Eskimo husband, on the other hand, offered his wife to a guest by means of the culturally sanctioned game of "Putting out the lamp." A good host was expected to turn out the lamp at night. This was an invitation for the guest to have sexual intercourse with the wife. The Ammassalik, however, became intensely jealous when his wife copulated with a guest in circumstances other than the lamp game or without a mutual agreement between two families to exchange mates. It was not unusual for the husband to kill the interloper.

> The Toda of Southern India, who were primarily polyandrous at the turn of the century . . . would consider the sequence of events described in the vignette to be perfectly normal. That is to say, the husband would not have been upset to find his wife having sexual relations again in the morning if the man were her *mokhthodvaiol*. The Todas had the custom of *mokhthoditi* which allowed husbands and wives to take on lovers. When, for instance, a man wanted someone else's wife as a lover he sought the consent of the wife and her husband or husbands. If consent was given by all, the men negotiated for the annual fee to be received by the husband(s). The woman then lived with the man just as if she were his real wife. Or, more commonly, the man visited the woman at the house of her husband(s).

> It is evident from these illustrations that the culture, far more than the individual, determines when one is to recognize threat and to experience stress.[20]

In most societies, men are allowed to have more than one partner. Psychologists Clellan Ford and Frank Beach report that in 84 percent of the 185 societies they studied, men were allowed to have more than one wife. Only one percent of the societies permitted women to have more than one husband. Most societies also look on "wife lending," "mate swapping," and extramarital sex more tolerantly than does American society.[21]

The new humanists point out that, traditionally, American society has strongly fostered marital permanence, exclusivity, and jealousy. Yet, in spite of the fact that their culture tells them they *should* be jealous of their mates, many American men are not. Kinsey and his associates found that if a husband learned about his wife's extramarital relations, his discovery caused "serious difficulty" only 42 percent of the time; 42 percent of the time it caused "no difficulty at all."[22] With a little effort, they argue, we can train ourselves to be far less jealous.

What does social psychology have to say about these questions? As you may recall from Chapter 1, we argue that both a person's mind and body make unique contributions to any emotional experience. Thus, if a society wished to suppress jealousy in its members, it could adopt either a mind or body strategy:

- *Mind:* Society could try to persuade people to label their feelings in a somewhat different way.
- *Body:* Society could try to arrange things so that the realization that we must share our "possession" with others would arouse a far less intense physiological reaction.

QUESTION

How can I control
my jealous feelings?

For some people, passionate feelings are more intense if they're fanned by a little jealous teasing. For others, however, jealousy is an uncontrollable, sometimes violent, emotion that can cause them great suffering. Recently, psychologists have set up a number of "jealousy clinics" to teach people to deal with this potentially destructive emotion. Here is the kind of advice they give.

Step 1: Try to find out exactly what it is that is making you jealous. Usually, something specific about the situation is bothering you. Are you upset because she's going out to lunch with someone else? Or is that perfectly okay? Is it that she's having sexual relations with someone? Or is that okay, too? Is it that now he probably thinks he's a better lover than you are? Or that she likes his jokes better than yours—she sort of smiles at yours and practically collapses at his? Is that it? Aha!

MISS PEACH by Mell Lazarus.
Courtesy of Mell Lazarus
and Field Newspaper Syndicate.

Key questions to ask are:

- What was going on in the few moments before you started to feel this way?
- What are you afraid of? What do you think is likely to happen to you if your partner continues the other relationship? What will happen to your partner?

Family therapist Larry Constantine lists several situations that often trigger jealousy. Think of the last time *you* were intensely jealous. Were any of the following responsible for your feeling that way?

- Feeling that you're no longer "number one" . . . and everyone knows it.
- Feeling upset because you can't predict what's going to happen.
- Feeling powerless. Realizing you can't control your partner . . . or your life.
- Being emotionally, sexually, or intellectually deprived.
- Feeling you've lost your privacy, territory, or exclusive access to your mate.
- Not having all the time with your partner that you'd like.[23]

The first step then is to understand what you feel and why you feel that way.

Step 2: Try to put your jealous feelings in perspective. Albert Ellis (Director of the Institute for Advanced Study of Rational Therapy) argues that jealousy has irrational and rational components: "When you are intensely or insanely jealous of your consort's extramarital affairs, you are almost always believing something like this: 'Isn't it *awful* that he or she is interested in someone else! I *can't stand* it! What an incompetent, what a slob I am for allowing him or her to get so absorbed elsewhere! And how can that ungrateful louse do a thing like that to me?' "[24]

Lovers who feel "awful" and "can't stand it" are suffering, in part, because they are childishly insisting on the unattainable. Is it really so awful that your partner is interested in someone else? Don't you have such longings? Is it true that you can't stand it? Or are you simply determined to feel utterly miserable if you can't get your way? Nobody gets everything they want; how you respond to deprivation is up to you. Why are you berating yourself for "slobbishness" and your mate for being an "ungrateful louse"? Are you playing it straight . . . or are you simply carrying on to get what you want? According to Ellis, we should and can abandon our irrational ideas.

There are, of course, also some rational reasons for feeling jealous: If your mate likes someone else more than you, it does say *something* about your desirability. And, if your mate falls desperately in love with someone else, he or she might actually leave you.

> If you care for someone, you will not want your relationship to be seriously jeopardized. And if this individual is thoroughly enjoying sex, love, companionable, professional, or other intense participations with one or more members of your own sex, why should you be deliriously happy about the relatively high probability of (1) your being alone when your partner is preoccupied with someone else; (2) his or her interest in you being considerably diluted; (3) your being at times sexually deprived when you are in a "let's-hop-into-bed" mood; (4) your having less of a living-together, sharing partnership than you previously had; and (5) your losing your partner entirely, in case he or she finds another consort more enjoyable or agreeable than you and decides to make him or her the main mate?[25]

Although you may never be able to eliminate jealousy from your life completely, you can gain some control over your feelings by forcing yourself to consider each jealousy-arousing situation more realistically. You can gain even more control if you can manage to change the situation.

Step 3: Negotiating a "contract." Once you know exactly what makes you jealous, you and your partner can begin to negotiate—to bargain toward a balance of security and freedom that you both find comfortable. Gordon Clanton and Lynn Smith suggest some ground rules that others experimenting with postmonogamous life-styles have found useful. Some of these rules contradict one another; this is simply because needs and values vary from couple to couple. You might wish to use this list to develop guidelines that are right for you and your partner.

- If there is ever a conflict between the needs of the primary and secondary relationships, the primary relationship gets the benefit of the doubt.
- Don't get sexually or emotionally involved without checking with me first.
- Do what you will, but don't tell me about it. And make sure the children and the neighbors don't find out.
- Outside experiences are all right, but emotional involvements are taboo. Keep it light.
- Outside sexual experiences are all right, but only with people you really care about.
- Only if I like the other person.
- Only if the other person is someone I don't know and won't meet.
- Only with single people.
- Only with people who are happily married and honest with their spouses.
- Only if I'm similarly involved.
- When one of us is out of town, we both do what we like.
- Not too often. (Be specific.)
- Tuesday night off. Each of us is entitled to some private time and space to spend as we will.
- I agree to wait a month before getting involved with _____ so we can work through some of the implications of this new relationship.[26]

A final note: Many counselors have found that it's a lot easier for couples to maintain a close—while not excessively possessive—love relationship if they each maintain some separate friends and interests. Naturally, it's easier to have confidence in your desirability if you have an independent identity and if there are others who like and admire you. You are far less likely to fear being abandoned by your partner . . . and it's a lot easier for you to cope if you are.

LONELINESS

No one has anything good to say about loneliness. It's a painful and frightening experience, linked to anxiety, social isolation, depression, and boredom. The lonely yearn for love and, frequently, if their yearning goes on too long, it gives rise to hate.

Like jealousy, loneliness is a common experience. In one national survey,[27] 26 percent of the Americans interviewed reported that they felt lonely and remote from others. Here's how one lonely woman described her feelings:

> I ache all over, inside and out, for this man. I drop all my own interests and activities and other relationships—even with my female friends—just to wait for him to call . . . and he never does. I'm always alone.
>
> When he calls, about once every two weeks, he usually calls late at night and wants to see me desperately, but mind you, *only* now—at 2:30 A.M. And, of course, I think he really wants to see *me,* so I take the flannel nightgown off and the hair curlers out—try to look as attractive as possible—only for him to say, "Wham-bam-thank-you-ma'am." But I find him so sweet and affectionate and intelligent—and good looking—that I'll sacrifice anything for him. And I rationalize his terrible behavior, his inconsiderate ways, until I drive myself crazy!!

Three UCLA psychologists have developed the following loneliness scale. How would you answer these questions?

LONELINESS SCALE [28]

For the following questions, you are to circle the choice that best illustrates how often each of the statements would be descriptive of you.

O = "I *often* feel this way."
S = "I *sometimes* feel this way."
R = "I *rarely* feel this way."
N = "I *never* feel this way."

1. I am unhappy doing so many things alone.	O	S	R	N
2. I have nobody to talk to.	O	S	R	N
3. I cannot tolerate being so alone.	O	S	R	N
4. I lack companionship.	O	S	R	N
5. I feel as if nobody really understands me.	O	S	R	N
6. I find myself waiting for people to call or write.	O	S	R	N
7. There is no one I can turn to.	O	S	R	N
8. I am no longer close to anyone.	O	S	R	N

9. My interest and ideas are not shared by those
   around me.   O   S   R   N

10. I feel left out.   O   S   R   N

11. I feel completely alone.   O   S   R   N

12. I am unable to reach out and communicate with
    those around me.   O   S   R   N

13. My social relationships are superficial.   O   S   R   N

14. I feel starved for company.   O   S   R   N

15. No one really knows me well.   O   S   R   N

16. I feel isolated from others.   O   S   R   N

17. I am unhappy being so withdrawn.   O   S   R   N

18. It is difficult for me to make friends.   O   S   R   N

19. I feel shut out and excluded by others.   O   S   R   N

20. People are around me but not with me.   O   S   R   N

Lonely people are in pain. It's no wonder, then, that they spend much of their time yearning for someone to love them. If they're involved in a bittersweet affair—sharing a few wonderful moments with someone they love, but most of their time alone—their feelings are probably even more volatile. They love their "on-again-off-again" mate for giving them so much (all that they have), but also hate him or her for giving them so little. For the lonely person, passion and loneliness may combine in an explosive kindling of devotion.

ANGER AND VIOLENCE

QUESTION

Is it normal to find that anger,
hostility, aggression, and fighting—instead
of turning you off—turn you on?

It's commonly believed that an angry person is a passionate person. We've all known couples who say that the best thing about having a big fight is making up in bed. And we've heard the perplexing stories of policemen or soldiers who go right from a gory shoot-out to lovemaking, without stopping to wipe off the blood. These stories embody an essential truth: anger *can* excite a sexual reaction.

Psychologist Andrew Barclay has done the most impressive research in this area. Barclay invited fraternity men and sorority women to compete in a creativity test. Dr. Barclay's assistant, a graduate of an exclusive Ivy League college, helped him administer the tests. In some groups (the calm and cool groups), the assistant was friendly and agreeable. In the remaining groups (the angered groups), the assistant was an obnoxious boor—arrogant, self-righteous, and bossy. His comments on fraternity men's and sorority women's intelligence and independence were scathing. After interacting with him for a few minutes, the participants were seething. When the assistant's instructions were complete, the experimenter entered and took over.

He asked the students to look at four Thematic Apperception Test (TAT) cards (a picture of a boss and a worker, a chess match, an instructor and student, and two lovers) and write imaginative stories about each picture. These TAT cards had been very carefully selected: two of the cards showed a powerful man hovering above a timid woman; two others showed a dominant woman tyrannizing a timid man.

Barclay was not really interested in the students' creativity, but in their sexuality. He speculated that the calm men and women should be just that: calm and collected. Angry men and women, on the other hand, should be volatile men and women—both emotionally and sexually. His predictions were confirmed.

The evidence that he was right came from two sources. First, the men's bodies gave them away. Normally, a man's prostate gland secretes acid phosphatase (AP) at a fairly constant rate. When a man becomes sexually excited, however, his AP secretion rate climbs precipitously. A physiologist can tell whether or not a man is sexually aroused by examining his urine. Sure enough, Barclay found that the angered men had far more AP in their urine than did the calm and cool men.

Second, the men's and women's fantasies gave them away. Barclay asked a team of psychologists to read through the men's and women's TAT stories and rate their "sexiness." As he expected, the angry men and women wrote far sexier stories (to appropriate pictures) than did their cool and collected counterparts. Angry men seemed to be turned on by dominant women; angry women by dominant men.[29]

Novelists—along with social scientists—have long observed how intimately interwined aggression and sex are in both animals and humans. Anger and aggression often precede and/or accompany sexual intercourse. Sigmund Freud argued that aggression and sex became linked during humankind's dim prehistory. In prehistoric times, only the most aggressive

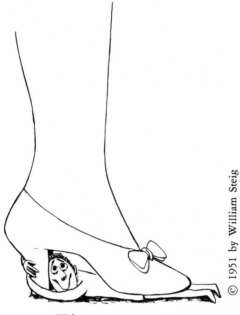

© 1951 by William Steig

What a woman!

and strongest men had a prayer of securing mates. As a result, aggression became inextricably linked to sex. Freud observed that, even today, sadism and masochism often stimulate sexuality.

Ethologists have amassed some support for Freud's notion. For example, male primates often signal their aggressive challenges—or their willingness to submit—via sexual means. A baboon troop posts guards in an area whenever it settles down to feed. The moment the guards sight another baboon troop, they issue a loud aggressive cry and make dramatic movements to call attention to their highly colored penises. In animals, it is often difficult to distinguish aggression/submission from a sexual encounter.[30]

In humans, aggression and sex are often similarly intertwined. Even our language reflects the close connection—for example, "Fuck you" or "I was screwed" (English); ¡Chinga tu madre!" ("Fuck your mother!") or "chucka" (cunt/damn) (Spanish); or "Kibaszott velem" ("He screwed up") or "Baszd ureg" ("Fuck it") (Hungarian).

—•◦◦◦•—
QUESTION
What about sadomasochism—is that normal?
—•◦◦◦•—

In the following typical interview, a New Yorker talks about his own and his friends' sadomasochistic experiences:

> *Everybody* is sadomasochistic.[31] The only difference between the man on the street and us is that we're daring enough to act out our fantasies. And that's what sadomasochism is—theatre.

> Peter is turned on by *very* light bondage. When he was young, he used to have these erotically tantalizing dreams about women with long, needle high heels—stepping, cruelly, on him. Now he's turned on by macho men—burly construction workers—tough, dirty motorcycle riders—and what not. Peter enjoys a little physical humiliation—but he's terrified of physical torture. I suppose the realization that these macho types might beat the hell out of him adds to his excitement.

> Some of my friends—like Jerry and Ed—are a little bit more serious. They like to give or receive enemas. These enemas always produce a bowel movement. If they're deeply inserted, they may cause pain, too. Sometimes they roll around in mud or oil.

> The main thing about SM is consent. I think that's why sadists are far rarer than masochists. You always think of the sadist in control, bending the helpless victim to his will. That's not true.

> It's the masochist who's in charge. It's his fantasies that get acted out. The point of sadomasochism is to put your life in the hands of a dangerous person and to survive; to trust him to do the terrible things he's promised—and only that.

When author Nancy Friday asked women to tell her about their fantasies, she found that sadomasochistic fantasies were surprisingly common:

> My husband has tried to get me to tell him about my sexual fantasies, but so far I have told him that I have none. It's almost as though he knew there was something or someone, in addition to himself, that was exciting me.

> These fantasies or dreams usually begin with my body being stretched, one brutal man on each limb, pulling me in opposite directions, literally spreading me wide open so that some immensely huge penis—there is no one or nothing on the end of it—begins to enter me, stretching me, rip-

Cordier & Ekstrom

While she is not a part of the leather scene, Nancy Grossman's sculptures of confined males are highly regarded by SM devotees.

ping me, my vagina, wide open as it pushes its way deeper into me. The men twist my arms painfully as well as pull them, and I can hear my bones breaking and cracking, while the sound of my skin, around my vagina, also rips audibly. I cry out in reality even as I cry out in my fantasy. But I love it, even though my intelligence and logic tell me that I am being ghoulish, that this is not a normal way to enjoy sex. And I do enjoy it. I hate what is happening to me in my fantasies, but it is inextricably involved with my very real pleasure.[32]

But is sadomasochism normal? That depends on your definition of "normal."

R. M. Suinn, for example, has proposed a very narrow definition of normality. He states: "The sexual deviations include all sexual behaviors in which gratification of sexual impulses is obtained by practices other than intercourse with a genitally mature person of the opposite sex who has reached the legal age of consent."[33] According to this definition, such common sexual activities as masturbation, fellatio, and cunnilingus would also be defined as "abnormal."

Byrne and Byrne propose another definition. They argue: "Abnormal sexuality consists of any sex-related behavior that causes psychological distress or unwanted physical pain for the individual engaging in the act and/or for an unwitting or unwilling participant."[34]

Thus, any sexual act is normal if the participants act knowingly and voluntarily, and if the act brings pleasure to both.

> If someone enjoys bondage, sadism, group sex, a partner of one's own sex, incest, masturbating with a vibrator or watermelon, dressing in the clothes of the opposite sex, working as a prostitute, becoming the customer of a prostitute, being urinated on, employing an unusual fetish object, or engaging in a heterosexual intercourse in the missionary position, he or she is behaving normally so long as all the conditions of the definition are met.[35]

If we agree with this definition, all impulses are perfectly normal—if one can find a willing partner. Any act is abnormal if any of the participants are unwittingly or unwillingly coerced into participation—or if it causes either of the participants unhappiness, remorse, discomfort, or physical injury.

> Thus, any violence or threat of violence or any force applied to coerce an unwilling victim are unacceptable. Any sexual act that takes advantage of another's weakness, fear, poverty, inexperience, ignorance, or state of consciousness is unacceptable—therefore sex with animals or children or someone who is mentally incompetent is not acceptable. Equally abnormal is sex with someone who is drugged, not in contact with reality, unconscious, or dead. Any sexual act that is unpleasant, anxiety provoking or guilt-inducing is unacceptable. Any sexual act which results in delayed negative consequences such as venereal disease or an unwanted pregnancy is unacceptable.[36]

Thus, whether or not an act is abnormal depends on the reasons for engaging in it, the feelings stirred up, and the outcome of the act.

Classified advertisements from a Berkeley, California newspaper.

MIXED EMOTIONS

QUESTION

Can you love and hate someone
at the same time?"

——————•◦◦◦•

Writers and artists have long been aware of the shadowy boundary between love and hate. In *Of Human Bondage,* W. Somerset Maugham expressed well this curious blend of conflicting emotions:

> When he lay in bed it seemed impossible that he should be in love with
> Mildred Rogers. Her name was grotesque. He did not think her pretty;
> he hated the thinness of her, only that evening he had noticed how the
> bones of her chest stood out in evening-dress; he went over her features
> one by one; he did not like her mouth, and the unhealthiness of her
> colour vaguely repelled him. She was common. Her phrases, so bald and
> few, constantly repeated, showed the emptiness of her mind; he recalled
> her vulgar little laugh at the jokes of the musical comedy; and he re-
> membered the little finger carefully extended when she held her glass to
> her mouth; her manners like her conversation, were odiously genteel.
> He remembered her insolence; sometimes he had felt inclined to box her
> ears; and suddenly, he knew not why, perhaps it was the thought of hit-
> ting her or the recollection of her tiny, beautiful ears, he was seized by
> an uprush of emotion. He yearned for her. He thought of taking her in
> his arms, the thin, fragile body, and kissing her pale mouth: he wanted
> to pass his fingers down the slightly greenish cheeks. He wanted her.[37]

Thirty years ago, Theodor Reik noted that one of the primary concerns that drove people to seek his psychiatric help was the enormous guilt
they felt when they realized how "abnormally" much they hated those they
loved. The clinical, animal-learning, child development, and social psychological literature reveals a curious but consistent finding: animals and men
are often attracted to those who are kindest *and* cruelest to them.

Let's consider just one example of this research. One scientist, in a
study using puppies, systematically varied how he treated the young animals. He treated two groups of puppies very consistently: he *always* responded to some of the pups with love and kindness; he *always* punished
some of the pups any time they dared to approach him. A third group of
puppies was treated in a very inconsistent way: sometimes they were
cuddled and petted; other times, for no reason at all, they were punished.
The results of this study were rather surprising. As it turned out, the

puppies treated inconsistently were most attracted to, and most dependent on, their trainer.[38]

This finding—and numerous others—suggests that ambivalence *is* a potent fuel for passion. Consistency generates little emotion; it is inconsistency that we respond to. If a person always treats us with love and respect, we start to take that person for granted. We like him or her—but "ho hum." Similarly, if a person is *always* cold and rejecting, we eventually tend to disregard his or her criticisms. Again, we know what to expect.

What would generate a spark of interest, however, is if our admiring friend suddenly started treating us with contempt—or if our arch enemy started inundating us with kindness. "What's going on here?" we'd wonder.

-------------•◊◊◊•-------------

QUESTION

Some sensible men and women
seem to be able to find just the right partners,
but I'm inevitably attracted to
the very lovers who are fascinating,
exciting . . . and impossible to live
with. Why is that?

-------------•◊◊◊•-------------

The juxtaposition of passionate love with ecstasy *and a*gony might not be entirely accidental. Although most people assume that we love the people we do *in spite of* the suffering they cause us, it may be that, in part, we love them *because* of the suffering they cause. Under the right conditions, anxiety and fear, insecurity, loneliness, frustration, jealousy, anger, and mixed emotions are all capable of fueling passion. Passion demands physical arousal and unpleasant experiences are just as arousing as pleasant ones.

The discovery that love flourishes when it's nurtured by a torrent of good experiences—and a sprinkling of unsettling, irritating, and even painful experiences—has some fascinating implications. Perhaps most important for us is the support it gives to the notion that a love affair fares best when lovers are relaxed and act naturally with one another. Women's "how-to-do-it" books—such as *Fascinating Womanhood* or *The Total Woman*—make a common mistake. Their authors understand Chapter 4's implications—that is, they encourage women to be attractive, agreeable, and to provide a pleasant environment for their men. But they totally miss the point of this chapter by not recognizing that a sprinkling of anxiety, jealousy, anger—of all the passions of life—is good for a relationship too. A loving relationship should be a complete emotional experience.

One word of caution: Obviously, there can be too much of a bad

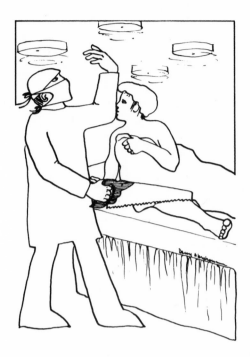

*Passion demands physiological arousal
and unpleasant experiences are arousing.*

thing. Early in a love affair, when we're living more on hope than on reality, a punishing lover—e.g., the hypercritical lover who is never satisfied with our appearance, our wit, or our heroic efforts to please; the overworked mate who is never home; the tense spouse who is "too busy" to share our problems; the brutal, psychopathic lover who screams at us or beats us—may convince us that "this must be love, because I feel so bad."

Later in the relationship, however, we lose hope and become less tolerant. We recognize that what we took for love would have been better labeled "humiliation," "disappointment," "anger," "rage," or "hatred." If you find yourself passionately attracted to a dangerous, exciting person who fills your life with pain only, stay away. In the not-so-long run, such relationships lose their passionate excitement and leave a residue of ugliness and pain.

six

How long does passionate love last?

The history of a love affair is the drama
of its fight against time.

Paul Geraldy, "L'Amour"

Is it not delightful to be in love? . . . It has happened to me twice.
It does not last, because it does not belong to this earth;
and when you clasp the idol it turns out to be a rag doll like yourself;
for the immortal part must *elude you if you grab at it.*

George Bernard Shaw
"To a Young Actress,"
letter of June 10, 1924

QUESTION

How long does love last?

Passionate love is characterized by fragility. Every lover always hopes that *this* love will last forever. But the rest of us, looking on, know that that's unlikely. Why is passionate love so short-lived? Our knowledge of passion gives us some clues as to why it so often ends in ashes. Earlier we learned that both our minds and our bodies have a critical impact on our emotions. However, in time, both our minds and our bodies change, and these changes dramatically affect our passionate feelings.

The change may take place in our minds. We begin to feel that, after so many years, it's not really appropriate to be passionately in love. Although there's strong cultural support for the notion that a man and woman *should* stay passionately in love forever, most of us have never heard of any couples who have.

The pattern that seems most common goes something like this: All newlyweds are romantic. The man is fiery, impetuous, and tender. The woman is soft, shy, and blooming. Somehow, in just a very few years, all that changes. The impetuous man turns into a dull, plodding businessman happier with his newspaper than with his wife. The blooming woman turns into a sharp-tongued shrew. We're all familiar with this dismal view of marriage and, to some degree, accept it as true. So, to some extent, one reason it's hard for a man and woman to stay passionately in love is that no one really expects them to. When cynics jeer at love, few object, and the long-married are more likely to nod in rueful agreement.

There's a second reason why passion so often ends in darkness, a reason linked this time to a change in our bodies:

> Love grows less exciting with time, for the same biological reasons that the second run on a fast toboggan slide is less exciting than the first. The diminished excitement, however, may increase the real pleasure. Extreme excitement is practically the same as fear, and is unpleasant. After the excitement has diminished below a certain point, however, pleasure will again diminish, unless new kinds of pleasure have meanwhile arisen.[1]

Thus, in time, our tumultuous feelings may subside. If we reexamine both the intensely delightful—and the intensely painful—experiences that originally ignited passionate love, we see that their intensity eventually flickers and dies.

108

*"Anything I would have done differently? Do you seriously want
to open that can of worms on your fiftieth anniversary?"*

THE DELIGHT OF PASSIONATE LOVE

LOVE: THE FANTASY

In time, even the most relentless of romantics is forced to realize that his
or her engaging fantasies have not been—and will not be—fulfilled. Early
in a love affair, our feelings toward a lover are kindled by the infinitely
rewarding experiences we can *envision* sharing. Once our life becomes
deeply intertwined with our partner's, our feelings are tempered by the
rewards—and punishments—we *actually* secure from this mere mortal.

Film stars Faye Dunaway and Catherine Deneuve both loved what
actor Marcello Mastroianni seemed to be. When they discovered the chasm
that existed between their fantasies and reality, they walked out. In an interview with Curtis Bill Pepper, Mastroianni observes:

> They told me, "I understand you as you are, as I have learned to know
> you . . . and you're not right for me. You appear to be sweet and gentle.

Instead, you're a monstrous egotist. You never alter anything in your private life—your rapport with your wife, children, friends . . . everything. With your smile and easy manner, you appear to be amenable to change. Instead, you play the game always according to your own rules. . . ." [He paused to sip some wine, then nodded.] That's what they said, and it's mostly true.[2]

LOVE: THE REALITY

Human beings rarely appreciate fully the things they have. How often do you appreciate the air you breathe? It's indispensable—but taken for granted. We only continue to appreciate the satisfaction of our needs if they are met *intermittently*.[3] The businessman who has worked twenty-five years for the same company and has received his check on time week after week takes it for granted he will be paid. If he were a worker in a fly-by-night company, he might greet each check with an immense sigh of relief.

Similarly, when a lover first comes along and fills the empty niches in our life, we feel passionately grateful. In time, however, we come to take both the giver and the gift for granted.

This discovery has some interesting implications for both our marital affairs and our extramarital ones. The man whose wife is *always* affectionate, or always has interesting anecdotes to tell him about her patients or legal clients, or always keeps the house immaculately clean eventually comes to take her assets for granted. The woman whose husband is *always* trustworthy, loyal, helpful, friendly, courteous, kind, obedient, cheerful, thrifty, brave, clean, and reverent . . . does the same. In time, they may not even be aware of the contribution their lovers make to their lives. (Of course, if their partners suddenly stopped doing these things, they would notice—and become enraged.)

What never fails to capture our attention are those things we want desperately—but can't have. Satisfied men and women have time to daydream about how permanently happy they would be *if* they had—whatever it is they don't have. He, for example, may start to brood because his wife—who is so wonderfully calm and efficient in the daytime—is equally controlled in bed; what he longs for *there* is a spontaneous, abandoned woman. She may realize that what she really wants is a poet. And so the cycle continues.

If either of them encounters a new lover—a person who promises to satisfy important, long-unfulfilled needs—he or she is likely to experience a strong stirring of emotions. Such delightful encounters provide the fuel for new passionate experiences. Of course, as soon as the new lover

"I'm so glad you're cynical. Roger was so full of hope."

begins to routinely satisfy *these* needs, new longings inevitably arise and the quest for a "perfect" lover is on once again.

Between Scylla and Charybdis

What we really want is the impossible—a perfect mixture of security and danger. We want someone who understands and cares for us, someone who will be around, through thick and thin, until we are old. At the same time, we long for sexual excitement, novelty, and danger. The individual who offers just the right combination of both ultimately wins our love.

The problem, of course, is that, in time, we get more and more security —and less and less excitement—than we bargained for from our love affairs. A poignant line from Frederick Raphael's *Two for the Road* says it all. A middle-aged man and woman are sitting together, staring, stone silent—in a romantic restaurant in the French countryside. A sparkling young girl who observes them asks her lover, " 'What kind of people just sit in a restaurant and don't say one word to each other?' 'Married people,' her lover answers." [4] The middle-aged couple's problem is not lack of love; rather, the problem is that each knows everything the other has to say. Often, they *can* literally finish one another's sentences.

In time, sex with the same person, in the same place, in the same way also loses its thrill. In *Professor of Desire,* Philip Roth describes the ebbing of his passion for Claire.

> Of course by now the passion between us is no longer quite what it was on those Sundays when we would cling together in my bed until three in the afternoon—"the primrose path to madness," as Claire once described those rapacious exertions which end finally with the two of us rising on the legs of weary travelers to change the bed linens, to stand embracing beneath the shower, and then to go out of doors to get some air before the winter sun goes down. We no longer *succumb* to desire, nor do we touch each other everywhere, paw and knead and handle with that unquenchable lunacy so alien to what and who we otherwise are. True, I am no longer a little bit of a beast, she is no longer a little bit of a tramp, neither any longer is quite the greedy lunatic, the depraved child, the steely violator, the helplessly impaled. Teeth, once blades and pincers, the pain-inflicting teeth of little cats and dogs, are simply teeth again, and tongues are tongues, and limbs are limbs. Which is, as we all know, how it must be.[5]

Roth is not alone. Doctors routinely warn middle-aged men who have suffered from a heart attack that, while they must shun their mistresses, it's perfectly all right to have intercourse with their wives.

> Whether a coronary patient should continue sexual activity is aptly summed up in a story of a recovering patient who questioned his physician in the matter. "By all means, have sexual intercourse," replied the doctor, "but only with your wife. I don't want you to become too excited." There is probably too much truth in that account for it to be humorous. A recent study of men with heart disease who died as a result of coitus revealed that 27 of the 34 deaths occurred during or after extramarital intercourse.[6]

In time, the wild delights of passion settle into accustomed pleasures.

PASSAGES

————•*ᴗᴗᴗ*•————

Love is the word used to label the sexual excitement
of the young, the habituation of the middle-aged, and
the mutual dependence of the old.

John Ciardi

————•*ᴗᴗᴗ*•————

There is a another reason why, in time, we appreciate less and less what
our lover has to offer. As we get older, what we want out of life changes.
In her insightful book *Passages,* Gail Sheehy points out that, in the perilous
ascent from youth to old age, we go through many stages. The things that
we find fulfilling in youth ("He's handsome; he has a Porsche." "She's
popular; she has her own apartment.") may not be so fulfilling later on.

Many psychologists[7] have observed that, as people approach and confront the inevitable crises in their lives, they change, sometimes in surprising ways. In *Passages,* Gail Sheehy describes some of the crises men and
women must confront in the course of their lives.

PULLING UP ROOTS (AGES 18–20)

At eighteen, we feel we have the potential to become anything. Teenage
girls often say such things as: "I can't decide whether to be sweet and shy
or sophisticated. What do you think?" Teenage boys don't know if they
want to go to college or quit school and make some big money now.

But what does the eighteen-year-old want to be? Usually, he or she
isn't really sure. But young adults *are* vehemently certain of what they
don't want to be (e.g., "I don't want to be a bored businessman like my
father"; "I don't want to be fat like my mother").

In this, as in every period, our *merger self* and our *seeker self* pull us
in opposite directions. Our merger self yearns to remain an infant, fused
with a warm, nurturing mother. We'll sacrifice anything for security—our
distinctiveness, our pride, our interests—anything. But our seeker self is
determined to become a unique individual, to explore our capacities, and to
become an independent person.

Sheehy points out that, until recently, both boys and girls solved the
dilemma of what to be by choosing to express only part of themselves. Boys
usually became seekers—denying any desire to merge. They escaped via the
military, college, or cross-country trips. Women generally tried to escape
the painful decisions of life by merging with a "strong one"—some man.

THE TRYING TWENTIES (20–27)

Early in our twenties, we make our decision. We decide who we are and what we want to be—for the moment at least. At eighteen, it seems as if these difficult choices are irrevocable. Thus, it becomes critically important to prove that our choices are the right ones—in fact, the only ones. We vehemently deny any evidence to the contrary.

Our vision of those we love is also distorted, built largely on illusion:

> Today, as then, it's enlightening to speculate on the degree to which a young man invents his romanticized version of the loved woman. She may be seen as the magical chameleon who will be a mother when he needs it and in the next instant the child requiring his protection, as well as the seductress who proves his potency, the soother of anxieties (who shall have none of her own), the guarantor of his immortality through the conversion of his seed. And to what degree does the young woman invent the man she marries? She often sees in him possibilities that no one else recognizes and pictures herself within his dream as the one person who truly understands. Such illusions are the stuff of which the twenties are made.

> "Illusion" is usually thought of as a pejorative, something we should get rid of if we suspect we have it. The illusions of the twenties, however, may be essential to infuse our first commitments with excitement and intensity, and to sustain us in those commitments long enough to gain us some experience in living.[8]

During our twenties, we devote all our time to doing the things we *should* do. At this time, Sheehy observes, men are generally initiators—the ones who seize the moment and push ahead to get what they want. They imagine that career success will make them immortal; they neglect their families. During this same period, women are generally responsive to other people's needs and wishes. They give their husbands unlimited love and support. They dutifully entertain his business contacts, make gourmet casseroles, sacrifice for their children. They imagine love will make them immortal; they neglect their own development. As men and women enter midlife, however, the tables begin to turn.

CATCH-30 (27–35) AND SWITCH-40 (36–45)

During our sensitive twenties, we are so uncertain of our fledgling identities that we bitterly resent any suggestion that there might be more to us than that. As we enter our thirties, however, we become increasingly sure of ourselves. We can drop our defenses a bit and admit to ourselves that some changes might be in order.

Now we become tired of doing all the things we *should* do and begin to feel an insistent urge to do what we *want* to do. We realize that, in devoting all our energy to living one pattern, we've harshly suppressed parts of ourselves. As one man approaching his thirties observed:

> What I've discovered over the last year is how much of what is inadmissible to myself I have suppressed. Feelings that I've always refused to admit are surfacing in a way *I am no longer willing to prevent.* I'm willing to accept the responsibility for what *I really feel.* I don't have to pretend those feelings don't exist in order to accommodate a model of what I should be. . . .

> I'm really shocked now at the range and the quality of those feelings—feelings of fear, of envy, of greed, of competition. All these so-called bad feelings are really rising where I can see them and feel them. I'm amazed at the incredible energy we all spend suppressing them and not admitting pain.[9]

In our late thirties, other changes propel us toward a midlife crisis.

• We are finally forced to face the truth we've suspected all along—we stand alone.

• We are stunned to discover that we are beginning to get old. Cracks appear in our physical shells. Grey hairs sprout. Our breasts begin to sag; our chests become crêpey. We find ourselves puffing on the racketball court. Even when we suck our stomachs in, we've lost our trim. We are ashamed.

• We realize time is running out. We realize with desperation that we must accomplish all that we can before it's too late, if it's not already too late.

Men and women may realize that the goals they have set for themselves are not attainable. They will never be president of the city bank. They will have to settle for becoming a branch manager in a suburban community. Theirs will not be the perfect family after all. Their children are already pushing to be off on their own. Even if they have been successful, they must now face up to a new problem: What next? What happens now that the dream's come true? If they don't replace it with a new dream, their energy, ambition, and zest for life are bound to deteriorate.

During this time, almost everyone who is married will also question that commitment. Men and women caught up in the throes of change frequently wish they could change partners or, at the very least, make them over entirely. When the traditional man selected his wife at age twenty-two, he may have been seeking a second mother. Now, however, his needs have changed; he wishes his wife would be a companion. "Why don't you take some courses?" he asks. Of course, he doesn't want her to get *too* interested in anything. If she suddenly announced her intention to become a lawyer, professor, designer, actress, or businesswoman, he would, no doubt, be alarmed. That would disrupt their lives too radically. But at least she could take some courses. Maybe they could move out of the city and buy a farm. Maybe they could move out of the suburbs and live in Manhattan . . . go to museums like they did when they were younger.

His traditional wife is in the throes of change too. She feels that she's spent the last fifteen years doing what her husband wanted; now it's time for him to sacrifice a bit for her. But he seems to be so preoccupied, so selfish. She wonders if she should have made different choices . . . given up family life for a career. Even if she had chosen differently, however, she would not have escaped a midlife crisis.

Margaret Hennig, a Harvard professor of business administration,[10] traced the lives of twenty-five women who were presidents or vice-presidents of large businesses and financial corporations. Interestingly, she found that they had remarkably similar life histories. Every one of the executives was a first-born child. Their fathers were crazy about them, thought they were talented, wonderful children. Father and daughter were comrades: they played tennis together, sailed together, went places together. Their fathers encouraged them to be independent. Their mothers were classic care-givers and tried to teach their daughters to be the same. But the daughters resisted. They did not see themselves as their mothers' competitors—they had won their fathers' devotion early on.

All the women went to college. After college, they went to work. There they met their mentors. The mentors took over where the fathers had left off: they loved them; they cheered them on; they supported them. When their mentors were promoted, they were promoted too; they could reveal all parts of themselves to their mentors.

Then they reached the age of thirty-five—and a midlife crisis. They realized that it was now or never. Did they want to continue to sacrifice everything for their careers? If so, they knew they must abandon their big-mentor/little-me relationships and begin to achieve on their own. Or, did they want to jump at their last chance to be a wife and mother? Hennig reports:

> All twenty-five took a moratorium for a year or two. They continued to work, but much less strenuously. With devil-may-care exuberance they all did things like buying flirtatious new wardrobes and having their hair restyled. They let themselves have fun again and freed time to enjoy the sexual part of their beings.

Almost half the women married a professional man they met during this period. Their nurturing side came into play too. Though none had natural children, all those who married became stepmothers.

The other half apparently did not meet anyone they could marry; when this momentous change caught them by surprise, they had literally no social life. But the fact of marrying or not marrying proved to make little difference. The women who remained single, no less than the others, realized they could not go on without making a basic shift in emphasis. They, too, became more outgoing, more responsive to people, and often, for the first time, were willing to become mentors themselves.[11]

After this short hiatus, all of the women returned to their goal of working toward top management. But their human connections became more honest and spontaneous. Earlier they had described themselves as "satisfied" or "rewarded." Now they added the word "happy."

RENEWAL

During their late forties and early fifties, men and women regain their equilibrium. A few of them have refused to face a midlife transition. Things will not go well for them. Their stale careers will become just jobs. They will see their parents become children, their children become strangers, and their mates go away or grow away. To stand still is to die.

On the other hand, if they've confronted themselves in the middle passage and found a renewal of purpose, these will be their best years. Their lives will become warmer and more mellow. Sheehy concludes: "Since it is so often proclaimed by people past midlife, the model of this stage might be 'no more bullshit.' "

SEXUAL PATTERNS

It's clear that we all undergo awesome changes during the passage from youth to old age. No wonder, then, that the lover who was all that we could hope for at eighteen may seem all wrong by middle age. "How did we ever get into this?" we wonder. But those aren't the only changes that occur.

Alfred Kinsey (and a host of latter-day Kinseys) have documented that men and women have very different sexual histories. At eighteen, it's usually the man who pushes to have sex. Boys are often given the double message of "Don't experiment sexually" and "Of course, a *real* boy never pays any attention to anything anyone tells him." As a consequence, most boys begin sexual exploration fairly early. Kinsey and his associates reported that most boys have begun to masturbate by age fifteen.

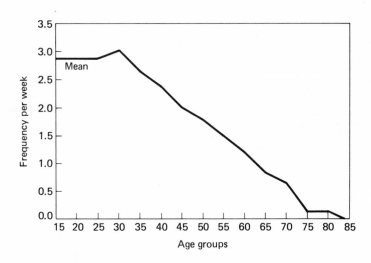

Frequency of total sexual outlet for males, by age groups.
(From A. C. Kinsey et al., *Sexual Behavior in the Human Male,* Philadelphia, Saunders, 1948, p. 220. Courtesy of the Institute for Sex Research.)

Society's message to women is far different: "Don't do it!" As a consequence, women are slow starters sexually. Most don't venture to try masturbation until they are in their later thirties. Further, once they begin to experiment sexually, their pattern of sexual activity looks quite different than that of men.

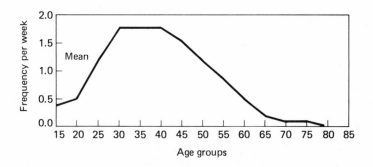

Frequency of total sexual outlet for females, by age groups.
(From A. C. Kinsey et al., *Sexual Behavior in the Human Female,* Philadelphia, Saunders, 1953, p. 548. Courtesy of the Institute for Sex Research.)

Kinsey and his colleagues set out to discover how sexually active men and women were throughout their lives. Their first problem was to settle on some quantifiable measure of "sexual activity." At eighteen, our sexual opportunities may be very different from those available to us at fifty. For example, although a fifteen-year-old boy may be very interested in having intercourse, he might have to settle for petting or masturbating simply because he can't find anyone who is willing to cooperate. By fifty, when he's stably married, he may do all his sexual experimentation with his wife. Thus, Kinsey and his colleagues developed a measure of "total outlets"— total sexual activity. They simply asked men and women how often they had an orgasm during a typical week—regardless of whether they achieved it by way of sexy dreams, petting, masturbation, sexual intercourse, homosexual encounters, or contacts with animals. They found that, indeed, men and woman do have strikingly different sexual histories.

Men are the most active sexually from age fifteen to age thirty. The popular notion that male sexuality is awakened during adolescence, gradually reaches its peak during the "prime of life," and then wanes is clearly a myth. A man is just as sexually expressive at fifteen as he will ever be.

In the teen years, men's erections become firm in a matter of seconds. Anything and everything can excite them. As they get older, it may take them a few minutes or more to get an erection. Many men begin to worry about losing their virility. Starting at age thirty, their sexual activity begins to decline steadily.[12]

William Masters and Virginia Johnson report that, in the United States, 25 percent of men are impotent by age sixty-five and 50 percent are impotent by age seventy-five.[13] A woman's experience is markedly different. At fifteen, women are quite inactive sexually. They have about one orgasm every three weeks. Sometime between the ages of sixteen and twenty, they slowly shed their early inhibitions and begin to feel enthusiastic about sexual exploration. They maintain this enthusiasm for a full decade. It is not until their late forties that sexual activity begins to ebb. In commenting on women's sexual histories, Kinsey observed:

> One of the tragedies which appears in a number of the marriages originates in the fact that the male may be most desirous of sexual contact in his early years, while the responses of the female are still undeveloped and while she is still struggling to free herself from the acquired inhibitions which prevent her from participating freely in the marital activity. But over the years most females become less inhibited and develop an interest in sexual relations which they may then maintain until they are in their fifties or even sixties. But by then the responses of the average male may have dropped so considerably that his interest in coitus, and especially in coitus with a wife who has previously objected to the frequencies of his requests, may have sharply declined.[14]

Thus, during many periods in their lives, men and women are bound to be responding to "different drummers" sexually.

In time, then, many of the delights that once fueled our passion dim, flicker, change, or disappear. If new delights do not replace them, and it is improbable that they will, we can expect our passionate feelings to dim, flicker, and die as well.

THE PAIN OF PASSIONATE LOVE

Love is a flickering flame between two darknesses. . . . Whence comes it?
. . . From sparks incredibly small. . . . How does it end? . . .
In nothingness equally incredible . . . the more raging the flame,
the sooner it is burnt out.

Heinrich Heine
Heine on Shakespeare (1895)

By now we know that a sprinkling of anxiety and fear, frustration, jealousy, or anger can intensify our passionate feelings. But what happens to these feelings with the steady dampening of time? It seems that, over time, the overwhelming and terrifying emotions—just like the delightful ones—spend themselves. Many people have written to us about their "bittersweet" experiences with love. We wondered what had become of these explosive affairs. So, we tracked down as many of our correspondents as we could and asked them how their relationships stood a year or two later.

ANXIETY AND FEAR

Salesman Jim Reynolds's early encounters with Helen were intensely painful for him. He was terrified that he might say the wrong thing or do the wrong thing during their fleeting encounters. Finally they met. As you might expect, the outcome was neither so wonderful nor so terrifying as he had anticipated:

> A terrible thing happened to us. We became friends. I discovered we both played racketball. . . . For awhile we played every Thursday night. At first it was wonderful. Our games were breathlessly erotic. . . . I'd brush up against her—she was always warm and glisteningly damp—and I could hardly keep my mind on the game. I kept drifting off into erotic daydreams.
>
> Usually, we'd go out for a drink afterward and talk. One night we were talking and I realized that instead of listening to Helen, I was

wondering if I had any clean socks to wear tomorrow. I was bored! . . .
Talking to Helen! That sort of killed things for me. We're still
friends, however.

SEXUAL FRUSTRATION

Freud, along with a host of ministers, high-school guidance counselors, and
hopeful parents, have warned adolescents that sexual frustration is the
foundation of romantic feelings. If sex were free, men and women would
have no need to idealize one another.

For the Victorians, the implications of this were clear: women should
save themselves for the men they love. A modern woman, however, drew
quite a different conclusion from this observation:

> The first time I saw Jim, I was determined to catch him. He was every-
> one's ideal man. He was good-looking, incredibly ambitious, and
> very, very competitive. He seemed to delight in ferreting out what
> other men secretly wanted, were working desperately hard to get, and
> showing that, with the flick of an eyelash, he could take it away from
> them. I found him irresistibly attractive.
>
> My mother warned me that I should never give into Jim. She'd say
> things like: "Once men get what they want, love disappears." So, I
> won. We got married. The only problem is, of course, that you're only
> a virgin once. She was right. After our wedding night . . . love did flee.
> So, what do I do now?
>
> A new mother in Flagtown, New Jersey

PARENTAL INTERFERENCE

A sixty-year-old woman reminiscing about her early marriage had this to
say:

> Before we were married, my mother hated Chuck. She did everything
> she could to keep us apart. I think that her main objection was that
> he wasn't Catholic. But there were other things too. He used to put a
> lot of pomade on his hair, and as he talked, he'd rub his head back
> and forth on the sofa. It made a big greasy ring there. My mother called
> him the "lounge lizard."
>
> And then, of course, she thought he was wild. He had a car and then
> nobody did. And when he'd go by our house he'd honk—his horn
> played "How Dry I Am." It embarrassed me, but I liked it too.
>
> My mother did everything she could to break us up. If I got back after
> 11:00, she'd lock me out. We'd have to knock to get back in; then

Passion rarely lasts for very long.

she'd scream at us from one of the upper windows. One night, we ran off and got married.

Immediately, everything changed. She started sort of flirting with him. She started getting him to do little jobs around the house; she became one of his staunchest supporters.

In time, the anxiety, fear, frustration, loneliness, and anger associated with courtship *do* spend themselves. Our feelings become less passionate, more tranquil. Of course, in any serious relationship, there is always a sprinkling of disturbing events to liven things up. Men and women find their desires thwarted ("He never wants to do anything on Saturday night but watch TV!"), they get jealous every now and then ("You were *so* dancing close to Phil!"), and they get upset when they find their partners' interest in them—and their interest in their partners—waning. These disturbing emotions tend to keep a marriage somewhat exciting. If painful experiences become too strong, however, they are more likely to produce hatred than renewed passion.

Conclusion: Passion rarely lasts for very long.

THE END OF THE AFFAIR

————•🐚🐚🐚•————

QUESTION

What happens to lovers when the passion
begins to fade?

ANSWER

Usually, they part.

————•🐚🐚🐚•————

Most passionate affairs end simply: the lovers find someone they love more. A few affairs end tragically. The lovers start out intensely committed to one another, but, in time, their feelings change. Passionate love erupts into ambivalence or hatred. Only over a period of time do these intense emotions cool to bearable indifference.

In the early 1970s, psychologists Zick Rubin, Anne Peplau, and Charles T. Hill studied 231 college couples for two years. At the beginning of the study, the typical couples had been dating for about eight months. Three-fourths of the couples were dating one another exclusively, but only 10 percent were engaged and relatively few had concrete plans for marriage. About four-fifths of the couples had engaged in sexual relations and about one-fifth were living together "all or most of the time." Sixty percent were seeing one another every day.

Two years later, only 128 of these couples were still dating; 103 of them had broken up. What caused the breakups? Although the details varied from one couple to another, David and Ruth's story is typical:

David and Ruth had gone together off and on for several years. David was less involved in the relationship than Ruth was, but it is clear that Ruth was the one who precipitated the final breakup. According to Ruth, David was spending more and more time with his own group of friends, and this bothered her.

She recalled one night in particular: "They were showing *The Last Picture Show* in one of the dorms, and we went to see it. I was sitting next to him, but it was as if he wasn't really there. He was running around talking to all these people and I was following him around and I felt like his kid sister. So I knew I wasn't going to put up with that much longer." When she talked to him about this and other problems, he said "I'm sorry"—but did not change.

Shortly thereafter Ruth wanted to see a movie in Cambridge and asked David if he would go with her. He replied, "No, there's something going on in the dorm!" This was the last straw for Ruth, and she told him she would not go out with him any more. David started to cry, as if the relationship had really meant something to him—but at that point it was too late.

At the time we talked to her, Ruth had not found another boyfriend, but she said she had no regrets about the relationship or about its ending. "It's probably the most worthwhile thing that's ever happened to me in my 21 years, so I don't regret having the experience at all. But after being in the supportive role, *I* want a little support now. That's the main thing I look for."

She added that "I don't think I ever felt romantic [about David]—I felt practical. I had the feeling that I'd better make the most of it because it won't last that long."[15]

Rubin found that very few of the breakups were *truly* mutual. Only 15 percent of the couples were equally eager to end things.

Interestingly enough, Rubin found that couples rarely agreed on how gradually (or abruptly) the breakup came about . . . or even on what caused it. The women tended to be very sensitive to the interpersonal problems involved and could identify them specifically: "We had conflicting ideas about marriage." "We had differences in intelligence." "Our interests were too divergent." "I wanted to be independent." "I was interested in someone else." Men tended to be less sure about what the problems were —they tended to see their problems as structural ones (e.g., "We lived too far apart").

FROM PASSIONATE LOVE TO COMPANIONATE LOVE

Passionate relationships don't always have to end. They can ripen into companionate love, "the kind of affection we feel for those with whom our lives are deeply intertwined."

Theodor Reik points out that, in some special relationships, love survives. After several years of loving, the passionate flame is transformed into a warm "afterglow."

A new kind of companionship, different from romance but no less valuable, may result in a sense of ease and harmony. Although idealization has ceased and passion has gone, yet the atmosphere is clear and calm. The lover has changed into a friend. There is no longer the violence of love, but the peacefulness of tender attachment.[16]

Most couples find, happily, that a friend is really what they needed all along. Anthropologists have argued that passion serves an important function in a marriage. Early in a relationship, a couple needs something—passion—to bond them together, while they chip away at the rough spots that exist in any relationship. By the time passion flickers out, it has been replaced by companionate love—shared understandings, emotions, and habits. Passionate love is a fragile flower; it wilts in time. Companionate love is a sturdy evergreen; it thrives with contact.

Scientists have found considerable support for this observation. A group of Colorado psychologists conducted an intensive study of both dating and married couples. They interviewed couples early in their relationships, and then again later. The researchers found that, at the beginning of a love affair, couples were romantically in love. As the relationships deepened, the "love" they expressed for one another began to sound less and less like passion—and more and more like friendship and companionate love.[17]

Passionate love is a fragile flower; it wilts in time. Companionate love is a sturdy evergreen; it thrives with contact.

Three other psychologists came up with exactly the same conclusion. The psychologists interviewed newlyweds to long-marrieds. They asked them to fill out Zick Rubin's "Passionate Love Scale" and his "Liking/Companionate Love Scale" (see Chapter 1).

The researchers found that the longer a couple had been married, the *less* passionately they loved one another:

Length of time married	Passionate love "score"
0 − 3 years	98.40
4 − 6 years	88.90
7 − 9 years	85.20
10 −17 years	84.04

However, over time, their scores on the companionate love scale remained uniformly high.[18]

Although passionate love loses its fight against time, companionate love does not. The friend/lover who shored up our self-esteem, shared our attitudes and interests, kept us from feeling lonely, reduced our anxiety, and helped us get the things we wanted early in the relationship continues to be appreciated many years later.

seven

Companionate love: you can't ~~always~~ *ever* get what you want

I said to Gloria, "You're always wishing for things you haven't got."
She said, "What else can you wish for?"

Buddy Ramsen[1]

A proposal of marriage in our society tends to be a way
in which a man sums up his social attributes and suggests
to a woman that hers are not so much better as to preclude a merger
or partnership in these matters.

Erving Goffman[2]

So far, we have explored the explosive mixture of emotions that is passionate love. We've learned that delightful as well as painful experiences can fan the flames of passion and that, eventually, these flames burn themselves out. Companionate love is different. It is a steady burning fire, fueled by delightful experiences but extinguished by painful ones.

In passionate love, we rush headlong into relationships with little or no thought for social convention or for how well "suited" we are for our partners. In companionate love, however, we are far more cautious. We are all on the lookout for a "perfect" mate . . . even though we know we may have to settle for something less.

What kind of long-term relationships do most people yearn for? What can we realistically expect to get out of a relationship? What must we be prepared to sacrifice? Scientists interested in companionate love have come up with some interesting answers to these questions.

QUESTION

What do men and women want in a love
partner?

Most of us think our own expectations for love partners are infinitely reasonable—in fact, modest. When a promising relationship falls through, we complain about the unfairness of it all. "I ask so little out of life," we lament. "All I want is someone to love me—and I can't even get that." We lie.

The moment we get down to specifics, it becomes clear that the "little" we ask is startlingly extensive. We want a good-looking person, a person with plenty of time to devote to us, a successful person, a sensitive person, a person with intelligence and a good sense of humor—the list goes on and on. Perfection is what we really want. "But that's not fair," you insist. "I'm not like that at all. I'm a warm, accepting, open person; I don't make impossible demands."

Let's see. Try an interesting experiment. Tomorrow, as you go about your daily activities, observe *everyone* you encounter—on the bus, on the street, at work, at school, at the supermarket. Keep a running total of those men or women you would be willing to date. You'll be startled to find out just how incredibly fussy you really are.

IT STARTS WITH OUR CULTURE

Every culture specifies who it is "appropriate" to date and marry. Without really thinking about it, most of us dutifully follow our culture's dictates;

128

in effect, we run a quick "criteria check" on every potential partner who happens our way. Most of us want partners of the opposite sex who are approximately our own age. They should be of our own race, socioeconomic class, religion, and educational level. They can't be too short or too tall. Such primary screenings cut out a surprising number of candidates.

How rigorous these initial screenings really are became all too evident to the existing computer dating companies when they began to calculate how many men and women they would have to enroll in their programs to accomplish the barest minimum of matching. These minimum requirements included matching individuals who:

- were of the opposite sex;
- lived in the same town;
- were of about the same age (What do you do when almost all your male clients are lonely thirty-year-old bachelors who want to meet some sexy girls, while your female clients are lonely fifty-year-old widows who want a second chance?);
- may want dates of the same race, socioeconomic class, religion, and educational level;
- were roughly the same height.

To its dismay, one computer company calculated that it would need more than one million subscribers in order to match on just these basic traits. So much for shared interests, sexual compatibility, and so on. (Interestingly enough, there is no computer-match company now in business with an enrollment figure even close to one million.)

THAT'S THE BEGINNING . . . BUT THERE'S MORE

Although we might start our search for a partner by seeking a "culturally acceptable" mate, we all expect a lot more. Recently, our colleagues—Jane Traupmann and Mary Utne helped us interview several hundred dating couples, newlyweds, and long marrieds to find out what they expected to give and to get from their relationships. Some of the replies were witty. One young woman simply picked up a Judith Viorst article and handed it to us:

> Brevity may be the soul of wit but not when someone's saying "I love you." When someone's saying "I love you," he always ought to give a lot of details: Like, Why does he love you? And, How much does he love you? And, When and where did he first begin to love you? Favorable comparisons with all the other women he ever loved also are welcome, and even though he insists it would take forever to count the ways in which he loves you, you wouldn't want to discourage him from counting.[3]

That was the kind of relationship she wanted.

A few replies were tragic: One Catholic said his wife had become an alcoholic. Recently, he had come home from work on a wintry day to find doors wide open, snow blowing in, and their three children wandering around the house undressed, unfed, and crying. On another occasion he'd found their infant daughter crawling in the street. All he expected from his marriage was a sober wife.

Most replies were perfectly ordinary: Many wives said they expected their husbands to support them. Many husbands said they expected their wives to keep the house clean and care for the children. Others expected their partners to be good-looking, successful, smart, considerate, calm (or emotionally expressive), sexy (or interested in far more than sex), religious, vegetarian . . . and on and on.

We ended up with a remarkable compendium of traits. Most men and women, however, agreed that the following assets were critically important in a date or mate. Go through the list now and check off those traits *you* think are critical.

Personal Contributions

Social grace
• Being sociable, friendly, and relaxed in social settings.

Intellect
- Being an intelligent, informed person.

Appearance
- Being a physically attractive person.
- Concern for physical appearance and health; giving attention to such things as clothing, cleanliness, exercise, and good eating habits.

Emotional Contributions

Liking and loving
- Liking your partner and showing it.
- Feeling and expressing love for your partner.

Understanding and concern
- Knowing your partner's personal concerns and emotional needs and responding to them.

Acceptance
- Accepting and encouraging role flexibility; letting your partner try out different roles occasionally—for example, letting your partner be a "baby" sometimes, a "mother," a colleague or a friend, an aggressive as well as a passive lover, and so on.

Appreciation
- Openly showing appreciation for your partner's contributions to the relationship; not taking him or her for granted.

Physical affection
- Being openly affectionate—touching, hugging, kissing.

Sex
- Participating in the sexual aspect of the relationship; working to make it mutually satisfying and fulfilling.
- Sexual fidelity; living up to or being faithful to your agreements about extramarital relations.

Security/freedom
- Committing yourself to your partner and to the future of your relationship together.
- Respecting a partner's need to be a free and independent person; allowing your partner to develop as an individual in the way that he or she chooses—for example, allowing your partner freedom to go to school or not, to work at the kind of job or career he/she likes, to pursue outside interests, to do things alone or with other friends, or simply to be alone sometimes.

Day-to-Day Contributions

Day-to-day maintenance
- Contributing time and effort to household responsibilities, such as grocery shopping, making dinner, house cleaning, and car maintenance.

Finances
- Contributing income to your "joint account."

Sociability
- Being a partner who is easy to live with on a day-to-day basis; that is, being someone with a sense of humor, who isn't too moody, doesn't get drunk too often, and so on.
- Being a good companion; suggesting interesting activities for the two of you to do together, as well as going along with your partner's ideas about what you might do for fun.
- Telling your partner about your day's events and what's on your mind; being interested in hearing about your partner's concerns and daily activities.

"If you want to talk, why don't you call up a radio talk-show?"

Published by Chronicle Books, San Francisco

*How about having a good
sense of humor?*

- Fitting in; being compatible with your partner's friends and relatives; liking them and trying to make them like you.

Decision making
- Taking your fair share of the responsibility for making and carrying out decisions that affect both of you.

Remembering special occasions
- Being thoughtful about sentimental things, such as remembering birthdays, your anniversary, and other special occasions.

Have we missed any characteristics that you think are critical? How about having a good sense of humor? Having someone who'll take you to a movie now and then without grumbling? Having someone who won't bring work home every night? Could you do without any of the traits mentioned?

It appears, then, that just falling in love is *not* enough for most of us. We start out wanting—and really expecting—an unrealistic degree of perfection in a partner. Implication: *We all want a lot more out of our relationships than we think we do.*

THE EQUITY THEORY [4] AND LOVE

---•✿✿✿•---

QUESTION

What is it *realistic* to expect
from a
relationship?

---•✿✿✿•---

We all feel that love relations should be very special kinds of relationships. Although we know full well that, normally, we spend most of our time seeking those things that make *us* happy—and avoiding those things that don't—we somehow feel that if we truly love someone, this selfishness should miraculously vanish. Suddenly, we should find ourselves acting selflessly, never concerned with what's in it for us. And, of course, we expect our lovers to feel a similar surge of selfless devotion. Isn't that what love's all about?

Many people have written to us expressing this viewpoint. Here's what a teacher from Rensselaer, New York, had to say: "An idea: There is real love and pseudolove. Real love is essentially religious in origin; it's irrational and based on faith; its chief component is caring for someone else. In contrast, pseudolove is materialistic, rational, and based on maintaining a favorable reward-punishment ratio. The other person is viewed as an accessory to oneself—necessary for self-expression and gratification."

A few psychologists—such as Erich Fromm, Judson Mills, Bernard Murstein, and Zick Rubin—also have argued that men and women are and should be unselfish in their love relations. But they are in the minority.

It's easy, of course, to see why people long to believe that love relationships are special relationships, relationships that transcend social exchange. Our yearning for unconditional love is a primitive one. We'd all like to believe that, even if we lost our looks, openly expressed our most unacceptable feelings, or refused to work, our lovers, family, and friends would continue to care for us.

The accumulating evidence, however, forces us to be more realistic:

- Men and women who insist that they are capable of dispensing love with no thought of return are simply deceiving themselves. Those who expect such selfless love from their partners most assuredly are.

- In fact, the more you are willing and able to give another, the more you can expect to get in return.

- Although we can *never* get exactly what we want, we can get the few things we want most.

We can gain some intriguing insights into the realities of love relationships by looking at a general theory of human behavior called "equity theory." It is based on four basic propositions:

1. People are biologically "set" to seek out pleasure and avoid pain. This biological trait is essential to human survival.

2. Society consists of a collection of selfish people. If society is to survive, its members must learn to compromise. They must accept the notion that you have to give a little to get a little, and that the more you give, the more you can expect to get.

3. People feel most comfortable when they're getting exactly what they feel they deserve in a relationship. *Everyone* in an inequitable relationship feels uneasy. While it's not surprising that deprived partners (who are, after all, getting less than they deserve) should feel resentful and angry about their inequitable treatment, it's perhaps not so obvious why their *over*benefited mates (who are getting more than they deserve) feel uneasy too. But they do. They feel guilty and fearful of losing their favored position.

4. Men and women who discover that they're in an inequitable relationship attempt to eliminate their mutual distress by restoring equity. They generally go about this in one of three ways:
  • They try to restore *actual* equity to their relationship.
  • They try to restore *psychological* equity to their relationship. (They try to convince themselves and others that their obviously inequitable relationship really is "perfectly fair.")
  • They also simply decide to end their relationship.

There is considerable evidence that equity theory affects whom we date, whom we live with, whom we marry, and how happy we are in our relationships. Let's look at some of this evidence.

WHOM WE DATE AND WHOM WE MARRY

Columbia sociologist Peter Blau observes that people end up with the mates they "deserve." If people hope to reap the benefits of associating with others, they must "make them an offer they can't refuse." The more desirable suitors are, the more desirable partners they can attract. Their less desirable fellows will have to settle for less desirable "leftovers." Thus, Blau argues, market principles ensure that people get the mates they deserve.

Men and women who possess one important asset—say, "physical attractiveness," or "intelligence," or "understanding and concern"—*are* likely to end up with an equally attractive, intelligent, or compassionate lover.[5]

Physical attractiveness

Several studies in the United States, Canada, Germany, and Japan show that women and men generally end up dating and marrying people who are just about as attractive as they are. Some of our own research has focused in this area.

In one project we organized a computer-matching dance for incoming freshmen at the University of Minnesota. When students appeared to purchase their tickets for the dance, four assistants who "just happened" to be sitting around the box office quickly rated their looks. Then we interviewed the students.

We found that the attractive men and women saw themselves as not just physically attractive, but as very attractive "total packages." They believed they had better personalities and were more popular and more outgoing than were their less-attractive counterparts.[6]

Others agreed with them. Pictures of the computer-match ticket-holders were shown to other students. These students were then asked, "What do you think these men and women are like?" Everyone seemed to take it for granted that these attractive men and women possessed every social asset imaginable. They were assumed to be more sexually warm and responsive, sensitive, kind, interesting, strong, poised, modest, sociable, and outgoing than their peers. They were also assumed to be more exciting dates, more nurturant, and to have better characters than "ordinary" people.[7]

A few days after the men and women signed up for the computer dance, they were assigned a date. The dance was held in a large armory. During intermission, we swept through the armory rounding up couples from the dance floor, lavatories, fire escapes—even adjoining buildings. We asked them to tell us frankly (and in confidence) what they thought of their dates. Six months later, we contacted all the individuals and asked them if they were still dating their computer matches. This experiment, and others like it, led us to several conclusions:

- All men and women—regardless of their own social desirability—agree about what's attractive. Ideally, they would all like to date breathtakingly beautiful (or handsome), personable, considerate people. How they actually behave, however, is another matter.

- Men and women don't expect perfect dates; they expect the all-knowing computer to select a date whose social desirability matches their own. Even when men and women are allowed to specify *exactly*

what they want in a date, they are hesitant to select anyone very different from themselves in social desirability.[8]

In another study, psychologists observed young couples in single's bars, in theater lobbies, and at social events. The physical attractiveness of the dates was rated from 1 to 5 in half-point intervals. The researchers found that 60 percent of the couples were separated by only half a point on the scale; 85 percent were separated by one point or less; and no couple was separated by more than 2.5 points.

The psychologists also hypothesized that the more similar two people were, the more delighted they would be with one another, and the more their delight would be reflected in intimate touching (such as holding hands, etc.). They were right. Sixty percent of the highly similar couples touched. Of the moderately similar couples, 46 percent were physically intimate. If couples were fairly dissimilar in appearance, only 22 percent of them ever touched.[9]

Other desirable traits

Physical attractiveness isn't the only asset that enables people to attract equally blessed partners. This holds true for other desirable characteristics as well. There is evidence that individuals who possess such assets as warmth, a dependable character, mental or physical health, a good income, intelligence, and so on have an especially good chance of "capturing" a lover with comparable assets.

Most clinicians agree that mentally healthy people tend to pair up, as do emotionally disturbed people. A psychoanalyst presents the case most strongly:

> All stories about a normal woman who becomes the prey of a neurotic man, and vice versa, or a normal man who falls in love with a highly neurotic woman, are literary fairy tales. Real life is less romantic; two neurotics look for each other with uncanny regularity. Nothing is left to chance as far as emotional attachments are concerned.[10]

Equity theorists, of course, would view this phenomenon quite differently. Both normals and neurotics may well desire well-adjusted partners. It may be the case, however, that only the normals are able to attract them, while neurotics must settle for partners as neurotic as themselves.

One psychologist asked engaged couples to complete several psychological tests and examined their scores. Six months later, he looked up the couples and asked them how their love affairs were going: Were they closer, the same, or further from becoming a permanent couple than before? He found that the more similar the partners' mental health, the more viable their relationship. Mentally healthy people ended up with partners as mentally healthy as themselves. Those who were a little crazy seemed to end up with partners who were a little crazy too.[11]

Sociologists Ernest Burgess and Paul Wallin conducted a classic study of the process of *homogamy* (the tendency for similar people to be drawn to each other). In a series of interviews, they discovered that engaged couples were very similar on almost every characteristic the researchers could think of. The couples matched up on:

- Physical appearance
- Mental health
- Physical health
- Family background (including race, religion, parents' status, educational level, and income)
- Family solidity (i.e., happiness of parents' marriage, etc.)
- Popularity[12]

MATCHING: MORE COMPLEX CASES

The research, as well as simple observation, makes it fairly clear that men and women tend to pair up with partners who possess similar traits. Lovers can be "matched," however, in a variety of ways. For example, a handsome man may use his assets to capture a beautiful woman—*or* he may decide to pursue a woman who is far plainer than himself, but is warmer and far more dependable than he is. An aging politician who proposes marriage to a young, attractive woman may be trading his prestige and power for her beauty and youth. There is compelling evidence that men and women do engage in such complicated balancing and counterbalancing in selecting mates.

WHAT BEAUTY CAN BUY

High socioeconomic status

In the 1930s, Oakland, California educators observed fifth- and sixth-grade girls as they cavorted on the school playground. Researchers rated the girls' facial beauty, coloring, figures, sex appeal, and grooming—in other words, their total appeal. Years later, sociologist Glenn Elder tracked down the girls to find out what had become of them. He found that the more attractive the preadolescent, the "better" she had done in securing a mate. The beautiful girls apparently used their beauty to capture mates whose social promise, and subsequent social power, far exceeded their own.[13]

MISS PEACH by Mell Lazarus.
Courtesy of Mell Lazarus and
Field Newspaper Syndicate.

High socioeconomic status + a loving nature + sacrifice

A recent *Psychology Today* questionnaire[14] asked readers to tell a little about their current dating, mating, or marital affairs. Sixty-two thousand readers replied.

"Who," readers were asked, "is the best looking—you or your partner? Describe your partner's physical attractiveness":

- Much more physically attractive than I.
- Slightly more physically attractive than I.
- As attractive as I.
- Slightly less attractive than I.
- Much less attractive than I.

Psychologist Ellen Berscheid and her Minnesota colleagues predicted that if couples were markedly mismatched on one dimension—say, physical appearance—there would be a compensating mismatch in other areas. They were right. The men and women who were more attractive than their partners admitted that their partners' assets balanced things out—for example, their partners were unusually loving or self-sacrificing or rich. Similarly, if the men and women were less attractive than their partners, they observed that it was they who possessed compensating assets.[15] It appears, then, that we can use our assets either to attract partners with exactly the same assets or to attract partners who possess quite different, complementary assets.

Although we prefer partners who are more desirable than ourselves, our actual choices are influenced by matching considerations. We all tend to end up with partners of approximately our own social value. Thus, our selection of a mate appears to be a delicate compromise between our desire to capture an ideal partner and our realization that we must eventually settle for what we deserve.

MISMATCHED RELATIONSHIPS ARE UNHAPPY RELATIONSHIPS

———◦◦◦◦———

In every love affair, there is one who loves
and one who permits himself to be loved.

W. Waller[16]

———◦◦◦◦———

But what happens when a person beats the odds? What happens when—through some fluke—people end up with dates or mates who are clearly superior (or inferior) to themselves? What happens when the prince marries Cinderella?

It's obvious, of course, why the prince might be dissatisfied: he can never really forget that he *could* have married a princess. But, Cinderella, his "lucky" mate, might have cause for unhappiness too, for she is confronted with a wrenching dilemma. On one hand, she is eager to keep the prince's love. After all, what are her chances of attracting so desirable a partner a second time? On the other hand, she is painfully aware that the prince has little reason to stay with her. Thus, both the "superior" and the "inferior" partner in an inequitable relationship might feel uneasy about their affair.

With our colleague Jane Traupmann, we decided to test the notion that equitable affairs are happier affairs. We interviewed more than 600 men and women, including dating couples, married couples, and couples living together.

Our first step was to try to find out whether or not the couple's relationship was a fair and equitable one. Using the checklist on pp. 130–133, we asked the men and women to consider how much they contributed to their relationships and how much they got out of them:

Considering what you put into your relationship compared to what you get out of it . . . and what your partner puts in compared to what he or she gets out of it, how does your marriage "stack up"?

   −3   My partner is getting a much better deal.
   −2   My partner is getting a somewhat better deal.
   −1   My partner is getting a slightly better deal.
    0   We are both getting an equal deal.
   +1   I am getting a slightly better deal.
   +2   I am getting a somewhat better deal.
   +3   I am getting a much better deal.

From this estimate, we could easily calculate how equitable the men and women perceived their love affairs to be.

We then asked the men and women, "When you think about your relationship—what you put into it and what you get out of it—how does that make you feel?" Specifically, we wanted to know:

- How *content* do you feel?
- How *happy* do you feel?
- How *angry* do you feel?
- How *guilty* do you feel?

We found that couples with equitable relationships were more content and happy than were other couples. Those men and women who knew they were getting far *more* than they really deserved were uneasy—they were less content, less happy, and a lot more guilty than were their peers. (It appears that lovers who are "too good" to their partners are really not doing them any favor.) Of course, those men and women who felt they were getting *less* than they deserved were in even worse shape—they were a lot less content, a lot less happy, and a lot angrier than were their peers.[17]

Is it true that couples in equitable relationships have better sex? No one knows for sure—at least, not yet. More sex? We decided to find out. We approached the dating couples we'd talked to earlier and asked them to tell us a little about their sex lives. "How far have you gone with your partner?" was our first question. Their answers included necking, petting, genital play, intercourse, cunnilingus, and fellatio. In addition, we asked those men and women *who had had sexual intercourse* to answer this questionnaire.

REASONS FOR ENTERING A SEXUAL RELATIONSHIP

People enter sexual relations for different reasons. Following are fourteen possible reasons for becoming sexually involved with someone. Check all of the reasons why you became sexually involved with your partner.

_____ 1. I was curious, wanted experience.

_____ 2. Partner wanted/needed it.

_____ 3. Mutual curiosity.

_____ 4. I wanted/needed it.

_____ 5. Partner wanted me to prove love.

_____ 6. We were/are in love.

_____ 7. To prove I am a man/woman.

_____ 8. I wanted to prove love.

_____ 9. We like/liked each other.

_____10. My friends think it is appropriate.

_____11. Partner convinced me it was appropriate.

_____12. Mutual physical desire, enjoyment.

_____13. I enjoyed it; it felt good.

_____14. Partner enjoyed it.

Three and one-half months later, we contacted the students once again and asked them to fill out an abbreviated version of the original questionnaire. As before, we asked them to estimate how intimate their relationships were. We found that couples in equitable relationships *do* have the most sexual relationships. Typically, they are having intercourse. Generally, men and women who feel they're "ripping off" their partners—or feel their partners are "ripping *them* off"—stop before "going all the way."

Couples in relatively equitable relationships usually agree that they had intercourse because they *both* wanted to (i.e., "Mutual curiosity"; "We are/were in love"; "We like/liked each other"; or "Mutual physical desire, enjoyment"). Couples in inequitable relationships are far less likely to say they both wanted sex.

THE DYNAMICS OF EQUITABLF/INEQUITABLE RELATIONSHIPS

What happens when a couple is seriously mismatched? What happens when the princess marries the frog, kisses him, and finds out that he really *is* only a frog after all?

The couple who discovers their relationship is precariously balanced will try to set things right in one of two ways:

- They may restore actual equity. The "superior" partner can demand better treatment; the "inferior" partner can begin to shower his or her mate with compensatory benefits.
- They may restore psychological equity. They can try to reassure themselves, their partners, and their friends that, really, things are fairer than they seem.

Restoration of actual equity

As one psychologist observed:

> There is an odd kind of equity which holds when people interact with each other. In effect, we get what we give, both in amount and in kind.

Each of us seems to have his own bookkeeping system for love, and for pain. Over time, the books are balanced.[18]

There is considerable anecdotal evidence that mismatched couples do try to "fine tune" their relationships. Frequently, when a person's physical appearance changes drastically—through accident, plastic surgery, or dieting—his or her expectations change too. For example, an article in *Weight Watchers* magazine warned readers that:

Marriage, like all relationships, is a balance. When one partner is overweight, that fact has been considered, perhaps unconsciously, in setting up the balance. Obviously, when you remove the obesity, you upset the balance. The relationship shifts and takes on a different complexion.[19]

Further, once excess weight is gone:

Gone are . . . the attempts to buy love through acquiescence and the overweight's traditional don't-make-waves-they-may-throw-you-out policy. In their place comes a new pride, an awareness of rights and a tendency to speak up for those rights.[20]

The Great Depression afforded Mirra Komarovsky a dismal opportunity to study the impact of dramatic changes in the marital balance. What happens, Komarovsky asked, when a man loses his job? Does he begin to lose authority?

During the winter of 1935–1936, Komarovsky contacted several dozen families who were receiving public assistance. In all the families, before the depression, the husbands had been the families' sole provider. When the depression hit, everything changed precipitously. The men lost their jobs and were forced to go on relief. Komarovsky interviewed both husband and wife to find out what impact, if any, this change had on their relationship. She found that, in 26 percent of the families, when the husband's ability to support the family disappeared, his authority did too.

Typically, two major kinds of changes occurred. In some families, the couples began to evolve a more egalitarian relationship. For example, in one family, for the first time, the man began to take on part of the household duties. In another family, a Protestant father who had forbidden his children to go to a Catholic school relented. In a few families, the status of husband and wife reversed. For example, in one case, a wife who had formerly treated her husband with careful respect now no longer bothered to be so polite. She began to harangue him for his inability to find work, to nag him constantly, to ignore his wishes, to argue with him, and to criticize him sharply, even in front of the children.

In another family, the husband observed: "There certainly was a change in our family, and I can define it in just one word—I relinquished power in the family. . . ." His wife agreed. She observed: "He still wants to be boss. This is his nature, even though he knows it wouldn't be for the best. He says he is treated like a dog in the house, but that's not true."[21]

Restoration of psychological equity

Of course, men and women sometimes find it harder to change their behavior than to change their minds. Sometimes couples, threatened by the discovery that their relationship is precariously balanced, prefer to close their eyes to the problem and reassure themselves that, "really, everything is in perfect order."

In intimate relationships, it's fairly easy to believe what you want to believe. Intimate relationships are complex relationships. Thus, even in the best of circumstances, couples often find it extremely difficult to decide what is fair. If couples expand their horizons and try to calculate how equitable or inequitable their marriages will be over the course of a lifetime, equity calculations become virtually impossible. Thus, when confronted with the fact that the balance of their marriage has changed, some partners find it easiest to try to convince themselves that, eventually, things will work out.

Often, they don't.

ENDING IT ALL

If a relationship becomes impossibly one-sided, the partners should be tempted to sever it. Obviously, it is far easier for dating couples than for married couples to end an affair. Most people feel that marital relationships should be enduring relationships; " 'Til death do us part" is still the cultural ideal. Dating couples who break up are likely to suffer, of course, but they will not experience the additional anxieties married couples face. Couples contemplating divorce realize that their parents and friends may be shocked, they may lose rights to their children, their close friends may drop them, their career opportunities may be affected. Further, it is expensive to secure a divorce and to establish and maintain two households.

Divorce, then, is costly in both emotional and financial terms. Yet, if a marital relationship is unbalanced enough, and if the partners can find no better way to resolve their differences, they may decide to separate. It has been estimated that 20 to 25 percent of first marriages end in annulment, desertion, or divorce.[22] In 1973, 913,000 couples opted for an annulment or a divorce.

*The more equitable a romantic
relationship is, the more viable
it will be.*

There is considerable evidence that the more equitable a romantic relationship is, the more viable it will be. Recently, we contacted a thousand
Wisconsin couples who were dating, living together, or married. We asked
them to answer these questions:

- How much do you contribute to your relationship?
- How much does your partner contribute to it?
- How much do you get out of your relationship?
- How much does your partner get out of it?

From the information they provided, we categorized the men and women
as:

- *Overbenefited:* All things considered, they feel they're getting a far
  better deal than their partners.
- *Equitably treated:* They feel they're getting exactly what they deserve.
- *Underbenefited:* They feel they're getting a far worse deal than
  their partners.

Three and one-half months after this initial interview, we got in touch
with the men and women once again to find out what had happened to

them. Equitable relationships do seem to be unusually solid relationships. Couples in fairly equitable relationships were the most likely to be seeing one another and to expect that they would still be seeing one another next year and five years later. Men or women who felt they were getting far less than they deserved from their affairs (and who had every reason to wish that something better might come along) were naturally quite pessimistic about the future of their relationships. But, so were those men and women who knew that they were getting far more than they deserved from their love affairs and thus had every reason to hope the relationship would last. They, too, had to admit that their affairs were fairly shaky.[23]

Equitable marriages may be stable marriages for yet another reason: such couples seem to be especially reluctant to risk getting caught up in a competing extramarital affair. The *Psychology Today* questionnaire we mentioned earlier also asked readers these two related questions about extramarital sex:

- When, after your present marriage, did you first have sex with someone else?
  1. Never
  2. Sixteen or more years
  3. Twelve to fifteen years
  4. Nine to eleven years
  5. Six to eight years
  6. Three to five years
  7. One to two years
  8. Less than a year

- With how many persons have you had sex during your present marriage?
  1. None
  2. One
  3. Two or three
  4. Four to ten
  5. Eleven to twenty
  6. Twenty-one to fifty
  7. More than fifty
  8. Not applicable

Their answers showed that the equitably treated and overbenefited men and women were very reluctant to experiment with extramarital sex. On the average, they were married twelve to fifteen years before they took a chance on getting involved with anyone else. Deprived men and women began exploring extramarital sex far earlier—approximately six to eight years after marriage. Similarly, the overbenefited had the fewest extramarital encounters (zero to one). Equitably treated men and women had a few more, and the deprived had the most extramarital liaisons of all (one to three).[24]

Equity theory, then, does provide a convenient model for examining romantic and marital relationships. Its principles do seem to determine whom we select as a date or mate in the first place; how we get along, day-to-day and thereafter; and how likely we are to stay together.

SOME PRACTICAL RECOMMENDATIONS

The discovery that equity principles guide our romantic relationships has some profound implications for how we should manage our lives. The more you have to offer—the more attractive, the more charming, and the more considerate you are—the more desirable a mate you'll be able to attract and hold.

... only God, my dear,
Could love you for yourself alone
And not your yellow hair.

W. B. Yeats
"For Anne Gregory"[25]

BEAUTY CAN BUY HAPPINESS...

We've all been told countless times from adolescence onward that looks don't count—it's what's *inside* that matters. But few of us ever bought that idea completely. Looks *shouldn't* count, of course, but we all know that they usually do. As we discussed earlier, social psychologists have accumulated file drawers full of evidence that good-looking men and women have a big advantage in the marriage market. Beauty does count.

BUT SO CAN INTELLECT,
SOCIAL GRACE, UNDERSTANDING, AND CONCERN

Earlier in this chapter, we listed the twenty-two things men and women care most about in a date or mate: social grace, intelligence, physical attractiveness, understanding and concern, and so on. This whole catalog of traits counts in determining your "worth" in the romance game. The more attractive you are as a total package, the more attractive a mate you can expect to attract and hold.

Beauty does count.

What are the implications of these findings? Let's focus on what you can do to make yourself as attractive a "package" as possible. First, become aware of what you have to offer. Figure out who you are. What are your four or five greatest strengths? (Think a long time about these.) What are your greatest weaknesses? (You can skim over these pretty lightly.)

Your goal is *not* to remold yourself so that you appeal to the "average" man or "average" woman—don't strive to be all things to all people. Your goal is to find that person (or those people) who will be unusually appreciative of your talents and unusually willing to tolerate your flaws. Find that someone who thinks it's very nice that you're extremely musical, have a good (if somewhat bizarre) sense of humor, and like to go for long walks in the evening; look for that someone who is willing to overlook the fact that you're not very good-looking, that you tend to be snappish in the morning, and that you're shy at parties. If you keep this simple goal in mind, you can avoid a lot of frustration and pain.

We've found that this advice is often a little hard to follow, since most of us are in the habit of viewing things the other way around: we assume something about us needs changing and, if we fix that, we'll be irresistible. This way of thinking is encouraged by women's magazines that, implicitly or explicitly, urge women to remold themselves to appeal to the "average" man—whoever that is. (He's the man who, "on the average," likes beautiful women . . . or gentle, submissive women . . . or women who are sexually accepting.)

But that's not what you want. You're not trying to remake yourself to appeal to "Mr. Average" or "Ms. Average"; you're looking for a special person to suit *you*. But, where can you find such men and women? Well, as we observed in Chapter 2, one way is to spend your time doing the things *you* like—playing the oboe with the New Original Hyperion Oriental Fox Trot Orchestra, contributing your slightly strange cartoons to a humor magazine, continuing to jog—very, very fast—through Central Park at night. And while you're there, keep an eye out for a person who seems to appreciate the same things.

So far we've spent all our time talking about how you can make the most of your assets. Now let's focus on the other half of the question: How can you find the man or woman who's the best possible match for you?

BEWARE OF WELL-MEANING ADVICE

Well-meaning marriage counselors advise people to exercise great care in selecting a mate. One counselor, for example, warns young men to use "logic and common sense" in choosing a wife. He advises them to make sure that their wives possess the following basic assets:

- Is beautiful.
- Is younger than you.
- Is shorter than you.
- Is the same religion.
- Is the same race.
- Is willing to pretend to be equally intelligent or less intelligent than you.
- Is a virgin at the time you meet.
- Is willing to live with you a year before marriage to see if things work out.

- Is willing to let you participate in the sports you like.
- Is tolerant of the work you do; is tolerant of your ambitions and abilities.
- Is willing to have as many sons as you want.
- Is sexually desirable.
- Is free from diabetes.
- Is not a regular drinker.
- Has not used marijuana, LSD, or similar drugs.
- Does not have a family history of insanity.
- Has large breasts.
- Has consent of both parents.
- Is a good cook.
- Is a good sewer and knitter.
- Is not a complainer or arguer.
- Is clean and neat.
- Is not overweight.
- Does not snore.[26]

Sound like good advice? Maybe . . . if you live in a storybook. For the rest of us, it's totally useless. This counselor is confusing fantasy with reality, assuming that, in a romantic relationship, you can always get what you want . . . if only you know what to look for.

There is a much better way to look at things. Give up the fantasy that you are entitled to an almost perfect mate. This fantasy is a destructive one. The "Standard American Male" and the "Standard American Female," equipped with all the virtues, simply do not exist. People come in a variety of packages, each with its unique blend of strengths and weaknesses.

What you should be looking for, then, is someone whose particular pattern of traits interlocks nicely with your own. You can select one or two —or maybe even a dozen—things you feel are critical to have in a mate. But then you have to quit. You must resign yourself to the fact that *any partner* is going to possess a multitude of less appealing traits. We're not telling you to give up your dreams; rather, we're encouraging you to become more aware of your own humanity and the delightful variety of partners, partly perfect and partly flawed, available to you.

One caution: Since you can only expect to get a few of the characteristics you want in a mate, you should think very carefully about what things are most important to you in a partner. Your society says the man you marry must be of your race and socioeconomic class, must be physically attractive, must want to get ahead professionally, and must be good at sports. That's something *it* cares about—but do you? Your mother says the woman you marry should be polite, neat, reliable, and put up with your Aunt Maude's quirks. That's something *she* cares about—but do you?

If you've not had very much experience, it is, of course, difficult for you to know exactly what you like and dislike in a partner. Be patient. The only sure way to discover what you care about is *via* experience. When you've had a chance to become deeply involved with many kinds of men and women, you'll discover that, with certain kinds of lovers, everything seems to go so well . . . while with others, life is impossible. When in doubt, ask yourself, "Is this the kind of person *I* want? Or is this the kind of person I've been told I should want?"

ASSESSING
YOUR RELATIONSHIP

QUESTION
How does my dating relationship
(marriage) "stack up"?

Granted, everybody gets something they want from their relationships—and, of course, they miss out on a lot as well. But maybe you're still curious. Maybe you're wondering exactly how your relationship compares to your neighbors'? Is your lover more, or less, understanding then others are? Is your husband or wife a more, or less, exciting sexual partner than are other husbands and wives?

Early in this chapter, we listed the things that men and women say they care about most in a relationship. We found that men and women have extremely high hopes for their relationships. But are these hopes realized? What do they actually get from their relationships? We decided to ask them. Here's how they responded to the question: "How rewarding is your relationship?"

	Never or not at all	Sometimes or moderate amount	Always or very much
	1 2 3	4 5 6	7 8 9

Personal Rewards

Social grace

- Having a partner who is sociable, friendly, and relaxed in social settings.

Intellect

- Having a partner who is intelligent and informed.

Appearance

- Having a physically attractive partner.

- Having a partner who takes care of his or her appearance and conditioning; who attends to such things as personal cleanliness, dress, exercise, and good eating habits.

Emotional Rewards

Liking and loving

- Being liked by your partner.
- Being loved by your partner.

Understanding and concern

- Having your personal concerns and emotional needs understood and responded to.

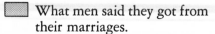 What men said they got from their marriages.

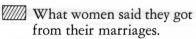 What women said they got from their marriages.

	Never or not at all			Sometimes or moderate amount			Always or very much		
	1	2	3	4	5	6	7	8	9

Acceptance

• Because of your partner's acceptance and encouragement, being free to try out different roles occasionally—for example, being a "baby" sometimes, a "mother," a colleague or a friend, an aggressive as well as a passive lover, and so on.

Appreciation

• Being appreciated for contributions to the relationship; not being taken for granted by your partner.

Physical affection

• Receiving open affection—touching, hugging, kissing.

Sex

• Experiencing a sexually fulfilling and pleasurable relationship with your partner.

• Sexual fidelity; having a partner who is faithful to your agreements about extramarital relations.

Security

• Being secure in your partner's commitment to you and to the future of your relationship together.

	Never or not at all	Sometimes or moderate amount	Always or very much
	1 2 3	4 5 6	7 8 9

Plans and goals for the future

- Planning for and dreaming about your future together.*

Day-to-Day Rewards

Day-to-day operations

- Having a smoothly operating household, because of the way you two have organized your household responsibilities.

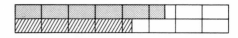

Finances

- The amount of income and other financial resources that you may gain through your "joint account."

Sociability

- Having a pleasant living-together situation, because your partner is easy to live with on a day-to-day basis.

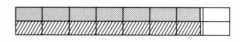

- Having a partner who is a good companion, who suggests fun things to do and who also goes along with your ideas for what you might do together.

- Knowing your partner is interested in hearing about your day and what's on your mind, and in turn will share concerns and events with you.

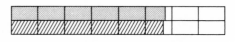

	Never or not at all			Sometimes or moderate amount				Always or very much	
	1	2	3	4	5	6	7	8	9

- Having a partner who is compatible with your friends and relatives; who is able to fit in.

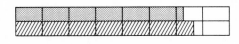

Decision making

- Having a partner who takes a fair share of the responsibility for making and carrying out decisions that affect both of you.

Remembering special occasions

- Having a partner who is thoughtful about sentimental things; who remembers, for example, birthdays, your anniversary, and other special occasions.*

Opportunities Gained and Lost

Opportunities gained

- Having the opportunity to partake of the many life experiences that depend on being married—for example, the chance to become a parent and even grandparent, the chance to be included in "married couple" social events, and, finally, having someone to count on in old age.

	Never or not at all			Sometimes or moderate amount			Always or very much	
1	2	3	4	5	6	7	8	9

Opportunities foregone

- Necessarily giving up certain opportunities in order to be in this relationship. The opportunities could have been other possible mates, a career, travel, etc.*

---

* In their preliminary report, Traupmann and Utne did not report how men and women rated their partners on these items.

How rewarding is *your* dating or marital relationship? How would *you* rate the rewards you get out of your relationship in these same twenty-four areas? Go ahead and try. You may gain some interesting insights into where your relationship is strongest and where it might need some improvement.

eight
Passionate and companionate love: making choices

Our discussion of passionate and companionate love leads us to a conclusion that is both heartening and disheartening: passion is a fragile essence. It provides joy, excitement, delirium, and fulfillment—along with anxiety, suffering, and despair—for a short time. Companionate love is a heartier flower. It can provide gentle friendship for life.

But humans are wily, difficult creatures. When faced with the question, "What do you want out of life—passionate love or companionate love?" we unfailingly answer, "Both."

Not only do we long for the impossible—we expect it. Somehow we harbor the hope that our life will be different from everyone else's. We may well recognize that passion is a fragile essence—that, in time, all relations settle down to a loving, but mundane, routine. Our parents, our friends, and the novels we read repeatedly remind us of this truth. So what? Our marriage will be different. Somehow we'll manage to maintain an intensely passionate, dramatic, tumultuous, breathtaking love affair—and, at the same time, share an easy, calm, stable existence with our partner.

No one, then, is willing to settle for passion or companionship alone. Everyone insists on a little of both. The real question, then, becomes: What *balance* of passion and companionship do you want from life? How highly do you rate the benefits of passion? Of companionship? To what extent are you willing to endure the costs of maintaining a passionate relationship? A companionate one?

CHOOSING THE PASSIONATE LIFE

Some people are determined to have a passionate life. They are willing to sacrifice more than most to get it. In every marriage, of course, there are passionate reawakenings. The excitement of a new job, the birth of a child, shared pleasures, momentous happenings all can reawaken passion. Such experiences are relatively rare, however. Some people insist on more.

WORKING TO KEEP A MARRIAGE PASSIONATE

A jumble of recent "how-to-do-it" books for women insist that if a wife is willing to exercise heroic effort, she can keep marital passion at a high pitch. Currently, the two supersaleswomen of this elixir are Helen B. Andelin (and her best-selling *Fascinating Womanhood*) and Marabel Morgan (*The Total Woman*). These counselors tell women that keeping passion alive is entirely the *woman's* problem.

First, they advise, women must learn to control their thoughts, emotions, and behavior. Ms. Morgan counsels women to learn "Total Submission." The wife must submit to her husband completely and unquestionably. She must learn to follow "The Four A's": to *accept* her husband by thinking only of his virtues and by forgetting his faults; to *admire* her husband and compliment his body; to *adapt* to her husband by living according to *his* schedule and tastes; and to *appreciate* her husband by being grateful to him and for him.[1]

Ms. Andelin tells women how they should go about controlling their thoughts, emotions, and behaviors. For example:

> What is childlike anger? . . . There is no better school for learning childlike anger than watching the antics of little children. . . .
>
> When such a child is teased . . . she stamps her foot and shakes her curls and pouts. She gets adorably angry at herself because her efforts to respond are impotent. Finally, she switches off and threatens never to speak to you again, then glances back at you over her shoulder to see if you thought she really meant it, only to stamp her foot in impatience when she sees that you are not the least bit fooled.
>
> One feels an irresistible longing to pick up such a child and hug it. . . .
>
> This is much the same feeling that a woman inspires in a man when she is adorably angry. This extreme girlishness makes him feel in contrast, stronger, and so much more of a man. . . .[2]

Last, but not least, women must employ an armory of little tricks to keep their husbands aroused. Ms. Morgan encourages women to inject "Super-Sizzle" into their marriages. She encourages them to greet their husbands at the door wearing pink baby-doll pajamas and white leather boots, to seduce them under the dining-room table, to slip mash notes in their lunch boxes, and to make breathy, suggestive calls to them at their offices. According to Ms. Morgan, the "rewards" for this activity include jewelry, refrigerators, rose bushes, luggage, wardrobes, nightgowns, furniture, and other items. Passion . . . plus.

The immensely popular sex manuals written by "J" (*The Sensuous Woman*) and "M" (*The Sensuous Man*) give similar advice:

> Ready for examples? Ted and Marge have been married eight years. The first three, Ted was insane about Marge in bed, but during the fourth year Marge became aware that Ted didn't devote as much time to sex. Where they used to spend maybe an hour making love, they now had somehow slipped back to about half an hour. If that wasn't ominous enough, Marge began to realize that their lovemaking had a set pattern. She knew everything Ted was going to do before he did it and what her response would be. . . .
>
> The next week Ted had to go to Pittsburgh on company business and, while he was away, Marge worked like a fiend. First she went to the

beauty salon and had her marvelous mane of dark brown hair streaked. Then she had their conventional bedroom done over in—are you braced for this?—mirrors. Smoky mirrors on the walls and ceiling. . . .

The day that Ted was due back from Pittsburgh, Marge called him and said she realized that he would be tired when he got home, but would he please, to humor her, follow exactly the instructions on the notes he would find in the apartment. Ted, his curiosity aroused, agreed.

The first note (on the door) read: "The fact that you're home makes me feel all warm and tingly. Put your suitcase down and go straight to the refrigerator."

The note on the refrigerator said: "Open the door and you will see a very dry martini in a prechilled glass. Take your drink to the guest bathroom."

In the bathroom Ted had instructions to soak in the tub of steaming hot water which was awaiting him, while he sipped his martini.

Scotch-taped to the towel he dried himself with was a note that said: "You have the most exciting body I have ever seen. If you want to see for yourself why you are the most sensual man in the world, come to the bedroom."

Ted, thoroughly intrigued (and pretty warm and tingly himself after the bath and martini), walked into the mirrored bedroom, caught sight of Marge stretched out on the fur throw in a black bikini, her body reflected, reflected, reflected everywhere and he flipped out. He never left that bedroom the whole weekend and he let Marge up only long enough to get food and drink occasionally.[3]

Faithfully follow *all* these tricks, the manuals promise, and your husband will never lose his "celestial love," or "tender caring," or "super-sex." Follow all these tricks and passionate love—as well as a generous helping of material rewards—will follow.

The love they guarantee is seductive:

When a man loves with all his heart there is a stirring within his soul. At times it is a feeling approaching worship for the woman. At other times he is fascinated, enchanted and amused. It has been described by some men as a feeling almost like pain. It can cause a man to feel like biting his teeth together. Along with all of these thrilling and consuming sensations, there is a tenderness, an overwhelming desire to protect and shelter his woman from all harm, danger and difficulty of life.

These feelings cause him to pour out his romantic love in words to her or to someone he trusts.[4]

"There! Do you still say 'the magic
has gone out of our marriage?'"

As exciting as all this sounds, social psychologists are skeptical at best. Their advice is: "Don't count on it." After a while, even the novelty of novelty wears thin.

SEARCHING FOR THE "EXTRA" IN EXTRAMARITAL RELATIONS

Some men and women pursue passion in extramarital relations: businessmen try to seduce the stewardess on the 12-minute hop from San Diego to Los Angeles; businesswomen engage in office flirtations—or fleeting affairs. Couples attend swinging parties. Long-time lovers huddle together on isolated beaches in the dead of winter or meet secretly over candle-lit dinners, in out-of-the-way art galleries, or in bed. At the same time, at home, these lovers maintain traditional, tranquil marriages with their spouses.

The decision to seek excitement outside of marriage (and security inside of marriage) is a common one. In the late 1940s and early 1950s, Dr. Alfred Kinsey and his colleagues interviewed more than 16,000 men and women and found that 50 percent of American men and 26 percent of American women had had extramarital affairs by the age of 40.[5]

In 1974, Morton Hunt reviewed the surveys that have been conducted in the quarter century since Kinsey's study. These surveys suggest that, paradoxically, not much has changed—and everything has.

Not much has changed
. . . everything has changed

Recent studies show that men are still engaging in extramarital sex with about the same frequency as in Kinsey's day. These same studies make it clear, however, that the double standard is dead or dying. Men *and* women have begun to look for the "extra" that comes with extramarital sex with about the same frequency. In Kinsey's day, only 8 percent of young wives —those under age twenty-four—had had extramarital sexual experience. In 1974, the Playboy Foundation found that 24 percent of young wives are now enjoying such encounters.[6] In addition, young marrieds are trying out some relatively new practices—mate swapping, swinging, and group marriage. The Playboy Foundation found that 2 percent of Americans— or 10.5 million—had tried swinging. Apparently, sizable numbers of Americans value the passionate experience and search for it outside of marriage.

Books that critique traditional marriage and discuss the pros and cons of alternative lifestyles (celibacy; staying single; agreeing on an open marriage; exploring homosexual affairs, bixual triads, swinging, group marriage, etc.) have suddenly become immensely popular. Two of the most celebrated of these are unquestionably Nena and George O'Neills' *Open Marriage* and the more recent *Shifting Gears*.[7] The O'Neills begin *Open Marriage* with a biting analysis of the traditional, closed marriage, an archetype familiar to us all. Men are supposed to be Standard American Husbands; women, Standard American Wives. If we don't fit tidily into the traditional mold—and none of us do—we are expected, like Procrustes of Eleusis, to lop off bits and pieces of ourselves until we achieve a perfect fit.

It is assumed that we will fulfill *all* our partners' needs—intellectual, psychological, emotional, and physical. The O'Neills observe: "This fantastic notion is blatantly unrealistic; an impossible dream." Like Siamese twins, we must always appear as a couple. We must loyally think the same thoughts, feel the same feelings, do the same things, share the same friends (couples, of course), and attend all cultural and social events together.

There is no archetype for the open marriage. Each couple must hammer out a "contract" for the kind of marriage that suits both partners. And, since each couple is unique, each contract will be different. Then, too, if a marriage is a vital one, it will be constantly growing and changing; thus, a couple's contract will be constantly evolving also to reflect these changes.

The O'Neills suggest a few guidelines for open marriages:

1. Both partners have unique identities. They have different values, capacities, expectations, and needs—not just because one of them is a man and the other is a woman—but because people are unique.

2. All men and women need someone with whom to share their deepest intimacies; someone they can trust and who will trust them in return. Thus, an open marriage requires open, honest, and free-flowing communication. Many traditional couples have the romantic idea that their partners should somehow be able to guess what they think, feel, and long for—and should magically be able to give it to them. This, too, is an unrealistic dream. Couples must confide in their partners and make a heroic effort to be honest.

3. Couples should work out agreements that suit *them*. When Jenny's mother comes to visit, Jenny will probably wish to spend considerable time with her. But should Jim? Not necessarily. That's something for both of them to work out. How much does she care? (Maybe she'd just as soon gossip with her mother alone. Or maybe she's dying to get Jim and her mother together.) What about Jim? How much does he care? (Would he like to visit with Jenny's mother? Or would he rather work on their income-tax return? Or sharpen his pencils?)

What if Barry is dying to go to a costume party and Sheryl is exhausted? Should they "compromise"—and end up doing what neither really wants to do? Why? Why shouldn't he stride off to the party, while she sits at home with a cup of tea and a good book?

4. Couples have the right to grow as individuals.

5. You cannot expect your mate to fulfill all your needs or to take care of you. Each person must accept responsibility for himself or herself and grant it to his or her mate.

6. Each person is entitled to enjoy new companions and experiences outside the marriage.

So far, so good—but when we get to the specifics of that last point, the controversy begins.

Open companionship/open love/open sex

Newlyweds are usually fully absorbed in one another; they have no time for others. But eventually, in a good marriage, couples come to love one another, understand one another, and feel deeply committed to one another. *Then,* the O'Neills argue, it's time for them to expand their horizons; to explore some activities suited just for them; to begin to develop other intimate friendships.

Fine, you say. But how intimate? Just friends? What if they meet someone who is better looking, smarter, richer, or more stimulating than their mate? Is it okay to get sexually involved with others? What about jealousy?

An open marriage can work, the O'Neills say, under certain conditions:

When a husband and wife have built for themselves an open relationship based on equality, honest communication, and trust, when their liking for one another, their love and respect for one another is defined by mutual understanding rather than by predetermined role structures or the coercive clauses of the closed contract, then the bond they form between themselves will be the central focus of their lives. Their own marriage will be their primary relationship. Precisely because this bond is so deep, so secure and so central to their lives, they can afford to open it up and let others in.[8]

Like Helene Andelin's promises, the O'Neills' promises are glittering. If you have an open relationship, they say, liking, mutual respect, and love will grow.

The benefits and costs of extramarital relations

First the good news. A roll call of the authorities who have come out in favor of extramarital sex is impressive: former president of the American Association of Marriage Counselors, Gerhard Neubeck; psychologist Albert Ellis; anthropologist Gilbert Bartell; novelist Robert Rimmer; psychologist Joyce Brothers; and a TV studio full of theologians, authors, actresses, and professional TV-talk-show guests.

Dr. Neubeck[9] points out that in a single love relationship, the chances of a couple feeling that all of their basic personality needs are being fulfilled are rather slim. There is scientific support for Dr. Neubeck's contention. In a study of 453 engaged or recently married persons, it was found that only 18 percent of them felt their emotional needs were "extremely" or "well" satisfied by their mates. The vast majority of men and women felt unloved, or lonely, or misunderstood.[10] On the other hand, if one has a *series* of love relationships, one can have different needs fulfilled in different relationships—and feel a different kind of love for different partners. Neubeck points out that such affairs benefit marriages by reducing the burden each mate places on the other.

In a session on the pros and cons of extramarital sexual relationships, psychologist Albert Ellis argued that most men and women have more to gain than to lose from adultery—and so do their mates. The benefits?

Sexual variety. Humans have a natural and biological need for sexual variety.

Desire for freedom. Many people find marriage satisfying but also confining. . . . When they get bored with steady marital routines, they find that engaging in outside affairs is one of the best ways to interrupt routines and add to their freedom.

Frustration reduction. Many individuals find monogamous mating limiting and frustrating, particularly when their mates do not have sexual appetites similar to their own.   .

Improved marriages. . . . Either or both married partners may feel less sexually and generally frustrated after an extramarital affair and thus less resentful toward each other. . . . They may be more open and honest with each other. Sex relations may improve along with greater appreciation of the partner.

Improved sex in marriage. Just as humans learn about sex in their premarital affairs, they will tend to learn about their own and others' sex proclivities in their extramarital relations. . . . This is especially true if the individual's premarital affairs had severe limitations. Extramarital sexual knowledge can be used to bring a more efficient and more enjoyable degree of sex to marriage.

Because adultery helps people, Ellis suggested removing legal barriers to extramarital unions, granting social sanction to those who engage in them, encouraging open marriage, and educating people to "cope more effectively with feelings of jealousy, self-downing, and other emotional problems that tend to accompany adultery today."[11]

And now for the bad news. In spite of the fiery rhetoric, itemizing the benefits to the individual and the marriage, extramarital arrangements do generate problems. Traditionally, we were all brought up believing that a "good" marriage is both *exclusive* and *permanent.* This belief is reflected in both religious and secular law. The *Book of Common Prayer,* for example, extracts the following promises from couples: "Wilt thou love her, comfort her, honor her, cherish her, and keep her; and forsaking all others, cleave thee only unto her, so long as ye both shall live?" and "Wilt thou love him, honor him, inspire him, cherish him and keep him; and forsaking all others, cleave thee only unto him, so long as ye both shall live?" The expected response, of course, is: "I will."

Americans—even those engaging in adultery—disapprove of it. The very words we use to describe extramarital sex—"cheating," "deception," "unfaithfulness," "running around," "playing around"—reflect our disapproval. The Playboy Foundation asked Americans how they felt about extramarital sex. ("Would you mind if your mate were to pet with another person?" "Were to have an occasional extramarital sex experience?" "Were to have an extramarital love affair?" "Would your mate object if *you* did any of these things?") The answer to each question was a resounding "yes." Anywhere from 80 to 90 percent said they (or their mates) would object to such activities.[12]

And, besides, it's against the law. Adultery—although rarely prosecuted—*is* a crime in 80 percent of the states. It's punishable by anything from a ten-dollar fine (in Maryland) to as much as five years' imprisonment in Maine, Oklahoma, South Dakota, and Vermont.

Given the traditional censure of extramarital affairs, it's not surprising that many modern couples—even those who carefully talk through their views on open marriage and conclude that they both *should* be free to grow and share their love with special friends—discover that they feel betrayed when their partner does, in fact, begin seeing another. Perfectly sensible men and women find themselves hysterically crying to friends on the phone, desperate for information about "him" or "her." Suddenly, they become painfully aware of just how much they love their mates. Intellectually, people may accept the fact that strangers often inspire more passion than do spouses. Emotionally, they never do.

Breaking up is hard to do

One real fear, of course, is that the "innocent" extramarital affair may lead to a shattered marriage. The extramarital partner may seem to be a far better match than the marital one. Or, the "betrayed" spouse may find it impossible to forgive his or her partner for doing the very things they agreed were perfectly okay to do—and ask for a divorce.

How likely is adultery to lead to trouble? Scientists don't know for sure. Kinsey and his colleagues concluded that adultery can be fairly harmless in a marriage—if the spouse doesn't find out.

How often do husbands and wives find out about their mates' extramarital affairs? Unfortunately, in collecting data for *Sexual Behavior in the Human Male,* Kinsey didn't bother to ask men whether or not their wives had discovered their infidelities or how they felt about them. By the time he got around to writing *Sexual Behavior in the Human Female,* though, Kinsey realized that these were important questions and asked them. About half of the women who had had affairs reported that their husbands had no inkling of them. About 9 percent of the women worried that their husbands might know and 40 percent were certain that they did know.

How did husbands react to these affairs? Kinsey found that when the man didn't know about the affair, it rarely precipitated trouble in a marriage. When he did know, there was "no" difficulty or "minor" difficulty 58 percent of the time. Only 42 percent of the time was there "serious" trouble.

Kinsey's conclusion: 71 percent of the time, extramarital relationships cause no marital trouble at all—either because the partners don't find out or because they don't care when they do.[13]

Psychologist John Gagnon wryly points out:

> In the Kinsey research there is a table, rather amusing because it is so self-serving. When people were asked, "Did *your* extramarital inter-

course figure in your divorce?" they answered one way. When they were asked, "Did your *spouse's* extramarital intercourse have any effect on your divorce?" they answered another. When *they* had the sex, they said it had very little effect on their divorce (though it might have if their spouse had known), but when they knew their *spouse* was having extramarital sex, it was viewed as a very important factor, especially by men.[14]

When scientists ask couples seeking a divorce what "caused" their breakup, included in their list of reasons is infidelity; in fact, it's one of the four main reasons that men cite for divorce.[15]

In brief, extramarital relations are a powerful lure. Although many "authorities" on marriage suggest that, by loving many partners, we can become more understanding, compassionate, playful, and complete people, extramarital sex is an elixir to be handled with caution. An ill-administered dose could prove fatal.

CHOOSING THE COMPANIONATE LIFE

Some people opt for early retirement from passion. They work hard to make their marriages as tranquil and companionate as possible. Such a choice has some real advantages, as well as some real disadvantages.

First the good news. A number of prominent authorities insist that the companionate way is the only way to happiness. Fundamentalist Billy Graham, radical Bishop Pike, Elliot Ness, Al Capone, every person who ever ran for office (including Wilbur Mills and Wayne Hays), and, of course, the man-on-the-street[16] all cast their votes for the companionate way of life.

EFFECT OF EXTRAMARITAL SEX ON DIVORCE

Question		Major effect	Moderate effect	Minor effect	No effect at all
Did *your* extramarital sex have any importance in causing your divorce?	(Women)	14%	15%	10%	61%
	(Men)	18%	9%	12%	61%
Did your *spouse's* extramarital sex have any importance in causing your divorce?	(Women)	27%	49%	24%	0%
	(Men)	51%	32%	17%	0%

Reprinted by permission from John H. Gagnon, *Human Sexualities* (Glenview, Ill.: Scott, Foresman, 1977), p. 220. Copyright © 1977 by Scott, Foresman and Company.

Some people opt for early retirement from passion.

And the companionate choice does have real benefits. Often, men and women get all the excitement they can handle at work, trying to be the most creative scientist, the most successful businessperson, or the most skilled athlete around. At home, they want to rest. A husband and wife often enjoy being able to count on the fact that, while their friends must contend with one emotional upheaval after another, *their* lives drift on in a serene, unruffled flow. They enjoy the fact that they can share day-to-day pleasures and that, in old age, they'll be together to reminisce and savor their lives. This portrait is very alluring.

And now for the bad news. The man or woman who chooses the companionate life must be prepared to endure certain costs, however. The relationship that is not fueled by at least some passion may ebb into a dull business exchange. Early in the marriage the partners establish a routine. And over the years they stick to it. They dutifully go to their jobs, care for their children and home. That's all. Nothing ever changes. They are not forced to acknowledge that both of them are complicated, exciting, ever-changing individuals—and they rarely do.

Many couples opt for such "no-relationship" relationships. Robert O. Blood and Donald M. Wolfe studied more than 900 marriages in the Detroit area. They interviewed a random sample of Detroit women to determine how satisfied the women were with their marriages. They found that most couples' marital satisfaction sags steadily with the passing decades: in the first two years of marriage, 52 percent of the wives were "very satisfied" with their marriages; none were notably dissatisfied. Twenty years later, only 6 percent were still "very satisfied;" 21 percent were conspicuously dissatisfied.

Blood and Wolfe suggest that two major factors contribute to marital deterioration in the later years. First, *disenchantment*—a cooling of enthusiasm—takes place with a shift from anticipation to fulfillment and from novelty to familiarity. Second, *disengagement* occurs—a progressive withdrawal of the couple from mutual interaction. As time passes, the partners spend less and less leisure time together—and when they are together, they pay less and less attention to each other. The authors conclude:

> Hence, corrosion is not too harsh a term for what happens to the average marriage in the course of time. Too many husbands and wives allow their marriages to go to seed for any milder term to be appropriate. As individuals, middle-aged husbands and wives may find satisfaction elsewhere —in friends, the husband in his work, the wife in her children—they seldom find as much in each other.[17]

THE TRADITIONAL CHOICE:
A PASSIONATE AND COMPANIONATE LIFE

So, far, the marital picture looks pretty dismal; both the passionate and companionate approaches to long-term love are fraught with difficulties. It is usually at this point that texts on marriage and the family offer "The Solution." They argue that people can solve the dilemma of passion versus companionship by arranging to have just the right mixture of both. They counsel readers to cherish those occasional sparks of passion that renew a marriage and to enjoy the steady companionship of day-to-day love. End of problem.

We would like *this* book to be a bit more honest. There is no universal answer to the problem of how to have a happy life. There is no single tried-and-true recipe for mixing just the right amounts of passion and companionate love into your marriage.

People change: their personalities change, their needs change, their bodies change. As they change, their desires change. The man who once thought he would sacrifice anything for passion may wake up one day to find that he's sick and tired of all the fuss. He wants what his friends have—a settled, companionate existence.

The woman who has always cynically disdained passion and has opted for a routine, calm, and stable life may discover that—in middle-age—she's changed her mind. She may find herself wildly attracted to a young man and conclude that passion is underrated and success and marital stability are overrated.

To make things more complicated, there are two people in a relationship—each moving through life according to his or her own rhythm. About the time a woman's children are leaving home and she is dying to begin a life of travel and excitement, her traveling-salesman husband may well be longing to become a homebody. A couple's desires are not always in phase. Life is unpredictable.

Life does not involve *one* choice, then, but a continuing series of choices. The arrangement a husband and wife work out one day may become untenable the next. Couples have to be prepared to negotiate and renegotiate what they want out of life and out of their relationships.

Life is unpredictable.

CONCLUSION

Moralists try to convince couples that if they live according to a few standard precepts, they can be guaranteed a happy life. This isn't true. No one can predict how a person, much less a marriage, will evolve. All a couple can do is choose what kind of life they would like to have and hope for the very best.

We can view the ever-shifting balance between passion and companionship in our lives either optimistically or pessimistically. We think there's much to be optimistic about. The realization that the future is unknown makes us feel alive. Today, more and more of us are becoming aware that loving relationships have unlimited possibilities—we can shape the future.

For the first time, men and women realize that the traditional male and female roles are not always satisfactory, nor is the traditional marriage relationship always a satisfying one for both partners. For the first time, men and women realize that they have the option of devising a marriage uniquely suited to their individual desires. They are free to make their needs known and to go after them. They are free to hammer out a uniquely pleasurable relationship with another. They can design a traditional marriage or an egalitarian one; she can work and he can tend the children, or they can live in a commune. Further, they are free to continuously redesign their lives as they change and mature. They have choices. Sound frightening? Of course. But the discovery is also an immensely exciting one.

Notes

CHAPTER ONE

1. S. Freud, reported in Theodor Reik, *A Psychologist Looks at Love* (New York: Farrar and Rinehart, 1944), p. 9.

2. S. Freud, Contributions to the psychology of love: a special type of object choice made by men (1910), reprinted in Philip Rieff, ed., *Freud: Sexuality and the Psychology of Love* (New York: Collier, 1963), p. 68.

3. T. Reik, *Of Love and Lust* (New York: Farrar, Straus and Cudahay, 1957), pp. 19–20.

4. Ibid., p. 109.

5. Ibid., p. 113.

6. Ibid., p. 114.

7. Ibid., p. 79.

8. Ibid., p. 33.

9. W. Griffitt, Environmental effects on interpersonal affective behavior: ambient effective temperature and attraction, *Journal of Personality and Social Psychology* 15 (1970):240–244.

10. A. H. Maslow and N. L. Mintz, Effects of esthetic surroundings: I. Initial effects of three esthetic conditions upon perceiving "energy" and "well-being" in faces, *Journal of Psychology* 41 (1956):247–254.

11. M. Argyle, *The Psychology of Interpersonal Behavior* (Baltimore, Md.: Penguin Books, 1967).

12. See, for example, E. Berscheid and E. Walster, *Interpersonal Attraction,* 2d ed. (Reading, Mass.: Addison-Wesley, 1978), pp. 1–20; or Z. Rubin, *Liking and Loving: An Invitation to Social Psychology* (New York: Holt, Rinehart, and Winston, 1973), pp. 222–225.

13. Sir Francis Galton, Measurement of character, *Fortnightly Review* 36 (1884): 179–185.

14. A. Mehrabian, Relationship of attitude to seated posture, orientation, and distance, *Journal of Personality and Social Psychology* 10 (1968):26–30.

15. D. Byrne, C. R. Ervin, and J. Lamberth, Continuity between the experimental study of attraction and "real life" computer dating, *Journal of Personality and Social Psychology* 16 (1970):157–165.

16. See, for example, A. E. Scheflen, Quasi-courtship behavior in psychotherapy, *Psychiatry* 28 (1965):245–257; or, N. Ashcraft and A. E. Scheflen, *People Space* (Garden City, N. Y.: Anchor Press/Doubleday), 1976.

17. Z. Rubin, *Liking and Loving: An Invitation to Social Psychology* (New York: Holt, Rinehart, and Winston, 1973), p. 215.

18. Reprinted from Z. Rubin, Measurement of romantic love, *Journal of Personality and Social Psychology* 16 (1970):267. Copyright © 1970 by the American Psychological Association. Reprinted by permission. Rubin labelled these scales the "Romantic Love Scale" and the "Liking Scale."

CHAPTER TWO

1. Copyright © 1951 Warner Bros., Inc. All rights reserved. Used by permission.

2. A. C. Clarke, An examination of the operation of residential propinquity as a factor in mate selection, *American Sociological Review* 17 (1952):17–22.

3. Reprinted from *Redbook* magazine, January 1977. Copyright © 1976 by The Redbook Publishing Company.

4. Ibid.

5. L. Festinger, Architecture and group membership, *Journal of Social Issues* 1 (1951):152–163.

6. R. B. Zajonc, Attitudinal effects of mere exposure, *Journal of Personality and Social Psychology: Monograph* 9 (1968):1–29.

7. From *How to Pick Up Girls!* by Eric Weber, pp. 92–93; copyright © 1970 by Eric Weber. By permission of Bantam Books, Inc.

8. H. G. Brown, *Sex and the Single Girl* (New York: Geis, 1963). Reprinted with the permission of Bernard Geis Associates from *Sex and the Single Girl*. © 1962 by Helen Gurley Brown.

9. Reprinted from *Shyness: What It Is, What to Do about It* by Philip Zimbardo, © 1977, by permission of Addison-Wesley Publishing Co., Reading, Mass.

CHAPTER THREE

1. Reprinted from J. A. Lee, The styles of loving, *Psychology Today,* October 1974, pp. 43–51. Copyright © 1974 Ziff-Davis Publishing Company.

2. Ibid., p. 48.

3. Ibid., p. 50.

4. Ibid., p. 51.

5. R. I. Levy, *Tahitians* (Chicago: University of Chicago Press, 1973).

6. R. Linton, *The Study of Man* (New York: Appleton-Century, 1936), p. 175.

7. W. M. Kephart, Some correlates of romantic love, *Journal of Marriage and the Family* 29 (1967):470–474.

8. Aristotle, *Nicomachean Ethics,* trans. by Martin Ostwald (New York: Bobbs-Merrill, 1962).

9. S. Firestone, *The Dialectic of Sex* (New York: Bantam Book/William Morrow, 1970), pp. 126–127.

10. C. W. Hobart, The incidence of romanticism during courtship, *Social Forces* 36 (1958):364. Copyright © The University of North Carolina Press.

11. E. J. Kanin, K. D. Davidson, and S. R. Scheck, "A research note on male-female differentials in the experience of heterosexual love, *The Journal of Sex Research* 6 (1970):64–72.

12. From Breakups before marriage: the end of 103 affairs, by Charles T. Hill, Zick Rubin, and Letitia Anna Peplau, in *Divorce and Separation,* to be published by Basic Books, Inc., Publishers, New York, in 1978. This article first appeared in the *Journal of Social Issues* 32, no. 1 (1976), edited by Oliver C. Moles and George Levinger, © 1976 by The Society for the Psychological Study of Social Issues.

13. S. de Beauvoir, quoted in Shulamith Firestone, *The Dialectic of Sex* (New York: Bantam, 1971), p. 135.

14. E. J. Kanin, K. D. Davidson, and S. R. Scheck, op. cit. With permission of *The Journal of Sex Research,* a publication of the Society for the Scientific Study of Sex.

15. W. Waller, *The Family: A Dynamic Interpretation* (New York: Dryden, 1938), p. 243.

16. A. R. Hochschild, Attending to, codifying and managing feelings: sex differences in love, paper presented to American Sociological Association, August 29, 1975, pp. 14–15. Reprinted by permission.

17. Ibid., p. 15.

18. J. Viorst, What is this thing called love? Reprinted from *Redbook,* February 1975, p. 12. Copyright © 1975 by the Redbook Publishing Company.

19. A. Ellis and R. Harper, *Creative Marriage* (New York: Lyle Stuart, 1961).

20. Z. Rubin, Measurement of romantic love, *Journal of Personality and Social Psychology* 16 (1970):265–273.

21. A. Cohen and I. Silverman, Repression-sensitization as a dimension of personality, in B. A. Maher, ed., *Progress in Experimental Personality Research,* Vol. 1 (New York: Academic Press, 1964), pp. 169–220.

22. From *How to Make Yourself Miserable,* by Dan Greenberg and Marcia Jacobs. Copyright © 1966 by Dan Greenberg. Reprinted by permission of Random House, Inc.

CHAPTER FOUR

1. S. Freud, Creative writers and daydreaming, in J. Strachey, ed., *The Standard Edition of the Complete Psychological Works of Sigmund Freud,* Vol. IX (London: Hogarth, 1962).

2. From *A Psychologist Looks at Love* by Theodor Reik, p. 43. Copyright © 1972 by Arthur Reik. Reprinted by permission of Holt, Rinehart and Winston, Publishers.

3. D. Parker, *The Portable Dorothy Parker* (New York: Viking Press, 1944), p. 180. Copyright © 1926, copyright renewed 1954 by Dorothy Parker. Reprinted by permission of The Viking Press. Copyright © 1973, National Association for Advancement of Colored People, by permission of Andrew D. Weinberger, Esq.

4. W. Stephan, E. Berscheid, and E. Walster, Sexual arousal and heterosexual perception, *Journal of Personality and Social Psychology* 20 (1971):93–101.

5. N. Friday, *My Secret Garden* (New York: Pocket Books, 1974), p. 2. Copyright © 1973 by Nancy Friday. Reprinted by permission of Simon & Schuster, a Division of Gulf & Western Corporation.

6. M. Hunt, *Sexual Behavior in the 1970's* (New York: Dell, 1974).

7. G. Schmidt, V. Sigusch, and S. Schafer, Responses to reading erotic stories: Male-female differences, *Archives of Sexual Behavior* 2 (1973):181–199; G. Schmidt and V. Sigusch, Sex differences in response to psycho-sexual stimulation by films and slides, *Journal of Sex Research* 6 (1970):268–283; and W. A. Fisher and D. Byrne, Sex differences and response to erotica: love versus lust, *Journal of Personality and Social Psychology* 36 (1978):117–125.

8. M. Hunt, *Sexual Behavior in the 1970's* (New York: Dell, 1974), pp. 88–98.

9. J. DeLora and C. Warren, *Understanding Sexual Interaction* (Boston: Houghton Mifflin, 1977), pp. 57–58.

10. Reprinted from *Redbook,* January 1977. Copyright © 1976 by The Redbook Publishing Company.

11. From *Love and the Loathsome Leopard* by Barbara Cartland, pp. 136–149. By permission of Bantam Books, New York, and Corgi Books, England. © 1977 by Barbara Cartland.

12. J. Bowlby, Affectional bonds: their nature and origin, in R. W. Weiss, *Loneliness: The Experience of Emotional and Social Isolation* (Cambridge, Mass.: MIT Press, 1973), pp. 44–45.

13. M. Zuckerman, The sensation-seeking motive, in B. Maher, ed., *Progress in Experimental Personality Research,* Vol. 7 (New York: Academic Press, 1974), p. 80.

14. M. Zuckerman, E. A. Kolin, I. Price, and I. Zoob, Development of a sensation-seeking scale, *Journal of Consulting Psychology* 28 (1964):477–481. Scale reprinted from *Dimensions of Personality,* H. London and J. Exner, eds., Sensation seeking, by Marvin Zuckerman. Copyright © 1978 by John Wiley & Sons, Inc.

15. Copyright © 1925 by e e cummings, reprinted from his volume *Complete Poems 1913–1962,* by permission of Harcourt Brace Jovanovich, Inc.

16. A. C. Kinsey, W. Pomeroy, and C. E. Martin, *Sexual Behavior in the Human Male* (Philadelphia: Saunders, 1948).

17. F. Beach and L. Jordan, cited in F. Beach, Copulation in rats, *Psychology Today,* July 1967, p. 58.

18. A. Fisher, cited in F. Beach, Copulation in rats, *Psychology Today,* July 1967, p. 58.

19. C. S. Blatt and R. C. Blatt, An evolutionary theory of social interaction, unpublished manuscript, 1970.

20. W. Griffitt, J. May, and R. Veitch, Sexual stimulation and interpersonal behavior: heterosexual evaluative responses, visual behavior, and physical proximity, *Journal of Personality and Social Psychology* 30 (1974), 367–377.

21. Sir R. Burton and F. F. Arbuchnot, trans., *The Kama Sutra* (New York: Putnam, 1964), p. 138.

22. E. Walster, G. W. Walster, J. Piliavin, and L. Schmidt, Playing hard-to-get: understanding an elusive phenomenon, *Journal of Personality and Social Psychology* 26 (1973):113–121.

CHAPTER FIVE

1. H. M. Halverson, Genital and sphincter behavior of the male infant, *Pedagogical Seminary and Journal of Genetic Psychology* 56 (1940):95–136.

2. F. K. Shuttleworth, A biosocial and development theory of male and female sexuality, *Marriage and Family Living* 21 (1959):163–170.

3. B. Russell, *The Autobiography of Bertrand Russell: The Middle Years 1914–1944* (New York: Bantam, 1969), pp. 18–19.

4. P. W. Hoon, J. P. Wincze, and E. F. Hoon, A test of reciprocal inhibition. Are anxiety and sexual arousal in women mutually inhibitory? *Journal of Abnormal Psychology* 86 (1977):65–74.

5. D. G. Dutton and A. P. Aron, Some evidence for heightened sexual attraction under conditions of high anxiety, *Journal of Personality and Social Psychology* 30 (1974):510–517 .

6. Ibid.

7. J. Galbraith, *The Ambassador's Journal* (Boston: Houghton Mifflin, 1969), p. 110.

8. S. Freud, Certain neurotic mechanisms in jealousy, paranoia, and homosexuality, in *Collected Papers, II* (London: Hogarth, 1922), p. 213.

9. Excerpted from "Artists and Models" in *Delta of Venus* by A. Nin, © 1977 by The Anais Nin Trust. Reprinted by permission of Harcourt Brace Jovanovich, Inc. Paperbook edition published by Bantam Books.

10. C. Rogers, Becoming partners, in *Marriage and Its Alternatives* (New York: Delta Books, 1972), p. 82.

11. R. Driscoll, K. E. Davis, and M. E. Lipetz, Parental interference and romantic love: the Romeo and Juliet effect, *Journal of Personality and Social Psychology* 24 (1972):1–10.

12. Simone de Beauvoir, *The Woman Destroyed,* trans. by Patrick O'Brian (New York: Putnam, 1967), pp. 136–137. Reprinted by permission of G. P. Putnam's Sons. Copyright © 1969 by Wm. Collins Sons & Co. and G. P. Putnam's Sons.

13. Ibid., pp. 193–195.

14. M. Mead, Jealousy: primitive and civilized, in A. M. Krich, ed., *The Anatomy of Love* (New York: Dell, 1960), p. 94.

15. K. Davis, Jealousy, *Social Forces* 14 (1936):395–405.

16. G. Clanton and L. G. Smith, *Jealousy* (Englewood Cliffs, N. J.: Prentice-Hall, © 1977), p. 11. Reprinted by permission of Prentice-Hall, Inc., Englewood Cliffs, New Jersey.

17. J. B. Bryson, Situational determinants of the expression of jealousy, in H. Sigall (Chair), *Sexual Jealousy,* symposium presented at the meeting of the American Psychological Association, San Francisco, August 1977.

18. C. Darwin, *The Expression of the Emotions in Man and Animals* (Chicago: University of Chicago Press, 1965).

19. E. Bohm, Is jealousy controllable? *International Journal of Sexology,* February 1952.

20. R. B. Hupka, Societal and individual roles in the expression of jealousy, in H. Sigall (Chair), *Sexual Jealousy,* Symposium presented at the meeting of the American Psychological Association, San Francisco, August 1977, pp. 7–9. Reprinted by permission.

21. C. S. Ford and F. A. Beach, *Patterns of Sexual Behavior* (New York: Harper & Row, 1951).

22. A. C. Kinsey, W. C. Pomeroy, C. E. Martin, and P. H. Gebhard, *Sexual Behavior in the Human Female* (Philadelphia: W. B. Saunders, 1953).

23. L. Constantine, Jealousy: Techniques for intervention, in G. Clanton and L. G. Smith, eds., *Jealousy* (Englewood Cliffs, N. J.: Prentice-Hall, 1977), pp. 190–198.

24. A. Ellis, Rational and irrational jealousy, in G. Clanton and L. G. Smith, eds., *Jealousy* (Englewood Cliffs, N. J.: Prentice-Hall, 1977), p. 173.

25. Ibid., p. 172.

26. G. Clanton and L. G. Smith, Synthesis: jealousy and intimate partnerships today, in Gordon Clanton and Lynn G. Smith, eds., *Jealousy* (Englewood Cliffs, N. J.: Prentice-Hall, © 1977), pp. 228–229. Reprinted by permission of Prentice-Hall, Inc., Englewood Cliffs, New Jersey.

27. N. Bradburn, *The Structure of Psychological Well Being* (Chicago: Aldine, 1969).

28. D. Russell, L. A. Peplau, and M. L. Ferguson, Developing a measure of loneliness, *Journal of Personality Assessment,* in press 1978. Used with permission.

29. A. M. Barclay, The effect of hostility on physiological and fantasy responses, *Journal of Personality* 37 (1969):651–667.

30. W. Wickler, *The Sexual Code* (Garden City, N. Y.: Doubleday, 1972).

31. There is *some* support for the speaker's contention. According to Paul Gebhard, Director of the Institute for Sex Research (the Kinsey Institute), 50 percent of men and women are aroused by being bitten. One in five men and one in eight women report that they find sadomasochistic stories arousing. See P. H. Gebhard, Fetishism and sadomasochism, in Martin S. Weinberg, ed., *Sex Research: Studies from the Kinsey Institute* (New York: Oxford University Press, 1976), pp. 156–166. Recently, Alex Comfort's best-selling *The Joy of Sex* (Fireside/Simon & Schuster, 1972) and *More Joy of Sex* (Fireside/Simon & Schuster, 1976) gave readers explicit scripts for acting out bondage, discipline and light sadomasochistic themes.

32. N. Friday, *My Secret Garden* (New York: Pocket Books, 1973), pp. 57, 123. Copyright © 1973 by Nancy Friday. Reprinted by permission of Simon & Schuster, a Division of Gulf & Western Corporation.

33. R. M. Suinn, *Fundamentals of Behavior Pathology* (New York: Wiley, 1970), p. 311.

34. D. Byrne and A. Byrne, *Exploring Human Sexuality* (New York: Crowell, 1977), p. 345.

35. Ibid., p. 346.

36. Ibid., pp. 345–346.

37. W. S. Maugham, *Of Human Bondage* (New York: Pocket Books, 1952), p. 159.

38. A. E. Fisher, The effects of differential early treatment on the social and exploratory behavior of puppies, Ph.D. dissertation, Pennsylvania State University, University Park, 1955.

CHAPTER SIX

1. J. K. Folsom, The romantic complex and cardiac respiratory love, *The Family* (New York: Wiley, 1934), p. 356.

2. M. Mastroianni, in Curtis Bill Pepper, Mastroianni talks about real life love, *Vogue,* October 1977, p. 124. Copyright © 1977 by the Condé Nast Publications, Inc.

3. R. Emerson, *Sociological Theories in Progress* (Boston: Houghton Mifflin, 1972).

4. F. Raphael, *Two for the Road* (New York: Holt, Rinehart and Winston, 1967), p. 71.

5. P. Roth, *The Professor of Desire* (New York: Farrar, Straus & Giroux, 1977), pp. 198–200.

6. J. L. McCary, *Human Sexuality,* 2d ed. (New York: D. Van Nostrand, 1973), p. 268.

7. Such as Erik H. Erikson, Else Frenkel-Brunswik, and Roger Gould.

8. Excerpted from *Passages: Predictable Crises of Adult Life* by Gail Sheehy. Copyright © 1974, 1976 by Gail Sheehy. Reprinted by permission of the publishers, E. P. Dutton.

9. Ibid., p. 361.

10. M. Hennig, Career development for women executives, Ph.D. dissertation, Graduate School of Business Administration, Harvard University, 1970.

11. Quoted in G. Sheehy, *Passages* (New York: Bantam, 1976), pp. 325–326.

12. A. C. Kinsey et al, *Sexual Behavior in the Human Male* (Philadelphia: Saunders, 1948).

13. W. H. Masters and V. E. Johnson, *Human Sexual Response* (Boston: Little, Brown, 1966).

14. A. C. Kinsey, W. B. Pomeroy, C. E. Martin, and P. H. Gebhard, *Sexual Behavior in the Human Female* (New York: Pocket Books, 1965), pp. 353–354.

15. From Breakups before marriage: the end of 103 affairs, by Charles T. Hill, Zick Rubin, and Letitia Anne Peplau, in *Divorce and Separation,* to be published by Basic Books, Inc., Publishers, New York, in 1978. This article first appeared in the *Journal of Social Issues* 32, no. 1 (1976), edited by Oliver C. Moles and George Levinger, © 1976 by The Society for the Psycholog cal Study of Social Issues.

16. From *A Psychologist Looks at Love* by Theodor Reik, p. 150. Copyright © 1972 by Arthur Reik. Reprinted by permission of Holt, Rinehart and Winston, Publishers.

17. R. Driscoll, K. E. Davis, and M. E. Lipetz, Parental interference and romantic love: the Romeo and Juliet effect, *Journal of Personality and Social Psychology* 24 (1972):1–10.

18. R. S. Cimbalo, V. Faling, and P. Mousaw, The course of love: a cross-sectional design, *Psychological Reports* 38 (1976):1292–1294.

CHAPTER SEVEN

1. B. Ramsen, My favorite jokes, *Parade,* July 17, 1977, p. 22. Reprinted by permission.

2. E. Goffman, On cooling the mark out: some aspects of adaptation to failure, *Psychiatry* 15 (1952):451–463.

3. J. Viorst, What is this thing called love? Reprinted from *Redbook,* February 1975, pp. 15–16. Copyright © 1975 by Redbook Publishing Company.

4. E. Walster, G. W. Walster, E. Berscheid, *Equity: Theory and Research* (New York: Allyn and Bacon, 1978).

5. P. M. Blau, *Exchange and Power in Social Life* (New York: Wiley, 1964).

6. E. Walster, V. Aronson, D. Abrahams, and L. Rottman, Importance of physical attractiveness in dating behavior, *Journal of Personality and Social Psychology* 4 (1966):508–516.

7. K. Dion, E. Berscheid, and E. Walster, What is beautiful is good, *Journal of Personality and Social Psychology* 24 (1972):285–290.

8. E. Walster, V. Aronson, D. Abrahams, and L. Rottman, Importance of physical attractiveness in dating behavior, *Journal of Personality and Social Psychology* 4 (1966):508–516.

9. I. Silverman, Physical attractiveness and courtship, *Sexual Behavior,* September 1971, pp. 22–25.

10. E. Bergler, *Divorce Won't Help* (New York: Harper and Brothers, 1948), p. 11.

11. B. I. Murstein, The relationship of mental health to marital choice and court-ship progress, *Journal of Marriage and the Family* 29 (1967):689–696.

12. E. W. Burgess and P. Wallin, *Engagement and Marriage* (Philadelphia: Lippincott, 1953).

13. G. H. Elder, Jr., Appearance and education in marriage mobility, *American Sociological Review* 34 (1969):519–533.

14. E. Berscheid, E. Walster, and G. Bohrnstedt, Body image, *Psychology Today* 6 (1972):57–66.

15. E. Berscheid, E. Walster, and G. Bohrnstedt, The body image report, *Psychology Today* 7 (1973):119–131.

16. W. Waller, The rating and dating complex, *American Sociological Review* 2 (1937):727–734.

17. E. Walster, G. W. Walster, and J. Traupmann, Equity and premarital sex, *Journal of Personality and Social Psychology* 37 (1978):82–92.

18. G. Patterson, *Families: Applications of Social Learning to Family Life* (Champaign, Ill.: Research Press, 1971), p. 26.

19. A. Jones, Marriage and the formerly fat: the effect weight loss has on your life together, *Weight Watchers,* March 1974, pp. 7, 23–50. Reprinted with permission of *Weight Watchers* magazine: "Weight Watchers" is a registered trademark of Weight Watchers, International, Inc. © March 1974; all rights reserved.

20. M. Palmer, in A. Jones, ibid.

21. M. Komarovsky, *The Unemployed Man and His Family* (New York: Octagon Books, 1971).

22. J. R. Udry, *The Social Context of Marriage* (Philadelphia: Lippincott, 1971).

23. E. Walster, G. W. Walster, and J. Traupmann, Equity and premarital sex, *Journal of Personality and Social Psychology* 37 (1978): 82–92.

24. E. Walster, J. Traupmann, and G. W. Walster, Equity and extramarital sexuality. *Archives of Sexual Behavior* 7 (1978):127–141.

25. W. B. Yeats, For Anne Gregory, *Collected Poems* (New York: Macmillan, 1941), p. 282. Copyright © 1933 by Macmillan Publishing Co., Inc., renewed 1961 by Bertha Georgie Yeats. By permission of Michael B. Yeats and Anne Yeats.

26. G. L. Herter, *How to Live with a Bitch* (Waseca, Minn.: Herter's, 1974).

CHAPTER EIGHT

1. M. Morgan, *The Total Woman* (New York: Pocket Books, 1973).

2. H. B. Andelin, *Fascinating Womanhood* (Santa Barbara, Ca.: Pacific Press, 1965), p. 180.

3. J., *The Sensuous Woman* (New York: Dell, 1969), pp. 86–88. Copyright © 1969 by Lyle Stuart, Inc.

4. H. B. Andelin, *Fascinating Womanhood* (Santa Barbara, Ca.: Pacific Press, 1963), p. 11.

5. A. C. Kinsey, W. B. Pomeroy, and C. E. Martin, *Sexual Behavior in the Human Male* (Philadelphia: Saunders, 1948); A. C. Kinsey, W. B. Pomeroy, C. E. Martin, and P. H. Gebhard, *Sexual Behavior in the Human Female* (New York: Pocket Books, 1965).

6. M. Hunt, *Sexual Behavior in the 1970s* (New York: Dell, 1974).

7. N. O'Neill and G. O'Neill, *Open Marriage* (New York: Avon, 1972); and *Shifting Gears* (New York: Avon, 1974).

8. N. O'Neill and G. O'Neill, *Open Marriage,* p. 173. Copyright © 1972 by Nena O'Neill and George O'Neill. Reprinted by permission of the publishers M. Evans and Company, Inc., New York, New York 10017.

9. G. Neubeck, *Extramarital Relations* (Englewood Cliffs, N. J.: Prentice-Hall, 1969).

10. Anselm Strauss, Personality needs and marital choice, *Social Forces,* March 25, 1947, pp. 332–335.

11. A. Ellis, Adultery may be beneficial, psychologist maintains. *Behavior Today,* 28 June 1976, p. 6. Published by Atcom, Inc., 2315 Broadway, New York. Subscription rate: $33/year.

12. M. Hunt, *Sexual Behavior in the 1970s* (New York: Dell, 1974).

13. A. C. Kinsey, W. B. Pomeroy, C. E. Martin, P. H. Gebhard, *Sexual Behavior in the Human Female* (New York: Pocket Books, 1963).

14. J. Gagnon, *Human Sexualities* (Glenview, Ill.: Scott, Foresman, 1977), p. 219.

15. For a review of this research, see G. Levinger, A social psychological perspective on marital dissolution, *The Journal of Social Issues* 32 (1976):21–48.

16. In *The Pleasure Bond,* Masters and Johnson explain, with proper scientific restraint, that they must be nonjudgmental—marital fidelity, affairs, swinging . . . it's all the same to them. But in "What Sexual Fidelity Means in a Marriage," their biases not only peep out—they blare forth. The traditional way is the only way.

17. R. O. Blood and D. M. Wolfe, *Husbands and Wives: The Dynamics of Married Living* (Glencoe, Ill.: The Free Press, 1960), p. 264.

Resources

GENERAL RESOURCES

Argyle, M. *The Psychology of Interpersonal Behavior*. Baltimore: Penguin Books, 1967.

Barclay, A. M. The effect of hostility on physiological and fantasy responses. *Journal of Personality* 37 (1969): 651–667.

Berlyne, D. E. *Conflict, Arousal, and Curiosity*. New York: McGraw-Hill, 1960.

Bernard, J. Infidelity: the moral and social issues. In Roger W. Libby and Robert N. Whitehurst, eds., *Renovating Marriage: Toward New Sexual Lifestyles*. Danville, Ca.: Consensus Publishers, 1973.

Berscheid, E., and E. Walster. Physical attractiveness. In Leonard Berkowitz, ed., *Advances in Experimental Social Psychology*. Vol. 7. New York: Academic Press, 1974, pp. 158–216.

Berscheid, E., and E. Walster. *Interpersonal Attraction*, 2d ed. Reading, Mass.: Addison-Wesley, 1978.

Bohm, E. Is jealousy controllable? *International Journal of Sexology*, February 1952.

Bowlby, J. Affectional bonds: their nature and origin. In R. W. Weiss, *Loneliness: The Experience of Emotional and Social Isolation*. Cambridge, Mass.: MIT Press, 1973.

Bryson, J. B. Situational determinants of the expression of jealousy. In H. Sigall (Chair), *Sexual Jealousy*. Symposium presented at the meeting of the American Psychological Association, San Francisco, 1977.

Burgess, E. W., and P. Wallin. *Engagement and Marriage*. Philadelphia: Lippincott, 1953.

Byrne, D. *The Attraction Paradigm*. New York: Academic Press, 1971.

Byrne, D., and A. Byrne. *Exploring Human Sexuality*. New York: Crowell, 1977.

187

Capellanus, A. *The Art of Courtly Love*. Introduction, translation, and notes by John Jay Parry. New York: Columbia University Press, 1941.

Clanton, G., and L. G. Smith. *Jealousy*. Englewood Cliffs, N.J.: Prentice-Hall, 1977.

Comfort, A. *The Joy of Sex*. New York: Crown, 1972.

Darwin, C. *The Expression of the Emotions in Man and Animals*. Chicago: University of Chicago Press, 1965.

Davis, K. Jealousy. *Social Forces* 14 (1936):395–405.

de Lora, J. R., and J. S. de Lora. *Intimate Lifestyles: Marriage and Its Alternatives*. 2d ed. Pacific Palisades, Ca.: Goodyear, 1975.

de Rougemont, D. *Love in the Western World*. Trans. by M. Belgion. New York: Harcourt Brace & World, 1940.

Dion, K., E. Berscheid, and E. Walster. What is beautiful is good. *Journal of Personality and Social Psychology* 24 (1972):285–290.

Driscoll, R., K. E. Davis, and M. E. Lipetz. Parental interference and romantic love: the Romeo and Juliet effect. *Journal of Personality and Social Psychology* 24 (1972):1–10.

Dutton, D. G., and A. P. Aron. Some evidence for heightened sexual attraction under conditions of high anxiety. *Journal of Personality and Social Psychology* 30 (1974):510–517.

Festinger, L., S. Schachter, and K. Back. *Social Pressures in Informal Groups: A Study of Human Factors in Housing*. New York: Harper, 1950.

Finck, H. T. *Romantic Love and Personal Beauty: Their Development, Causal Relations, Historic and National Peculiarities*. London: Macmillan, 1902.

Firestone, S. *The Dialectic of Sex*. New York: Bantam/William Morrow, 1970.

Folsom, J. K. The romantic complex and cardiac respiratory love. *The Family*. New York: Wiley, 1934, pp. 68–76.

Friday, N. *My Secret Garden*. New York: Pocket Books, 1974, p. 2.

Freud, S. Contributions to the psychology of love: a special type of object choice made by men (1910). In *Collected Papers*. Vol. 1. New York: Basic Books, 1959.

Goode, W. J. The theoretical importance of love. *American Sociological Review* 24 (1959): 38–47.

Hochschild, A. R. Attending to, codifying and managing feelings: sex differences in love. American Sociological Association, August 29, 1975.

Hunt, M. *Sexual Behavior in the 1970's*. New York: Dell, 1974.

Jones, E. E. *Ingratiation: A Social Psychological Analysis*. New York: Appleton-Century-Crofts, 1964.

Kanin, E. J., D. K. D. Davidson, and S. R. Scheck. A research note on male-female differentials in the experience of heterosexual love. *The Journal of Sex Research* 6 (1970): 64–72.

Kephart, W. M. Some correlates of romantic love. *Journal of Marriage and the Family* 29 (1967): 470–474.

Kinsey, A. C., W. Pomeroy, and C. E. Martin. *Sexual Behavior in the Human Male.* Philadelphia: Saunders, 1948.

Kinsey, A. C., W. C. Pomeroy, C. E. Martin, and P. H. Gebhard. *Sexual Behavior in the Human Female.* Philadelphia: Saunders, 1953.

Lee, J. A. The styles of loving. *Psychology Today,* October 1974, pp. 43–51.

Libby, R. W., and R. N. Whitehurst. *Marriage and Alternatives: Exploring Intimate Relationships.* Palo Alto, Ca.: Scott, Foresman, 1977.

Masters, W. H., and V. E. Johnson. *Human Sexual Response.* St. Louis: Brown, Little, & Brown, 1966.

Murstein, B. I. *Who Will Marry Whom? Theories and Research in Marital Choice.* New York: Springer, 1976.

O'Neill, N., and G. O'Neill. *Open Marriage.* New York: Avon, 1972.

Ovid. *The Art of Love.* Trans. by R. Humphries. Bloomington: Indiana University Press, 1957.

Patterson, G. *Families: Applications of Social Learning to Family Life.* Champaign, Ill.: Research Press, 1971.

Reik, T. *A Psychologist Looks at Love.* New York: Farrar & Rinehart, 1944.

Rubin, Z. *Liking and Loving: An Invitation to Social Psychology.* New York: Holt, Rinehart & Winston, 1973.

Russell, B. *Marriage and Morals* (New York: Bantam, 1968).

Russell, D., L. A. Peplau, and M. L. Ferguson. Developing a measure of loneliness. *Journal of Personality Assessment,* submitted.

Schachter, S. The interaction of cognitive and physiological determinants of emotional state. In Leonard Berkowitz, ed., *Advances in Experimental Social Psychology.* Vol. 1. New York: Academic Press, 1964, pp. 49–80.

Sheehy, G. *Passages.* New York: Dutton, 1976.

Singer, J. L. *Daydreaming: An Introduction to the Experimental Study of Inner Experience.* New York: Random House, 1966.

Thurber, J., and E. B. White. *Is Sex Necessary?* New York: Harper & Brothers, 1929.

Waller, W. The rating and dating complex. *American Sociological Review* 2 (1937): 727–734.

Walster, E., G. W. Walster, and E. Berscheid. *Equity: Theory and Research.* Boston: Allyn & Bacon, 1978.

SPECIALIZED RESOURCES

Abrams, R. H. Residential propinquity as a factor in marriage selection. *American Sociological Review* 8 (1943): 288–294.

Adams, B. N. *The Family: A Sociological Interpretation.* Chicago: Rand McNally, 1975.

Allgeier, A. R., and D. Byrne. Attraction toward the opposite sex as a determinant of physical proximity. *Journal of Social Psychology* 90 (1973): 213–219.

Andelin, H. B. *Fascinating Womanhood.* Santa Barbara, Ca.: Pacific Press, 1963.

Ankles, T. M. *A Study of Jealousy as Differentiated from Envy.* Boston: Bruce Humphries, 1939.

Arnold, M. B. *Emotion and Personality.* Psychological Aspects, vol. 1. New York: Columbia University Press, 1960a.

Arnold, M. B. *Emotion and Personality.* Neurological and Physiological Aspects, vol. 2. New York: Columbia University Press, 1960b.

Arnold, M. B. *Feelings and Emotions.* New York: Academic Press, 1970.

Aronson, E., and D. Linder. Gain and loss of esteem as determinants of interpersonal attractiveness. *Journal of Experimental Social Psychology* 1 (1965): 156–171.

Aserinsky, E., and N. Kleitman. Regularly occurring periods of eye motility and concomitant phenomena, during sleep. *Science* 118 (1953): 273–274.

Azrin, N. H., B. J. Naster, and R. Jones. Reciprocity counseling: a rapid learning-based procedure for marital counseling. *Behavior Research and Therapy* 11 (1973): 365–382.

Backman, C. W., and P. F. Secord. The compromise process and the affect structure of groups. In C. W. Backman and P. F. Secord, eds., *Problems in Social Psychology.* New York: McGraw-Hill, 1966.

Baron, R. A., and T. A. Bell. Effects of heightened sexual arousal on physical aggression. *Proceedings of the Annual Convention of the American Psychological Association,* 1973, pp. 171–172.

Baron, R. A., and D. Byrne. *Social Psychology: Understanding Human Interaction.* 2d ed. Boston: Allyn and Bacon, 1977.

Bartell, G. D. Group sex among the Mid-Americans. *Journal of Sex Research* (1970): 113–130.

Beach, F. A. A review of physiological and psychological studies of sexual behavior in mammals. *Physiological Review* 27 (1947): 264–265.

Beach, F. A., and B. J. LeBouef. Coital behavior in dogs. I. Preferential mating in the bitch. *Animal Behavior* 15 (1967): 546–558.

Bell, R., S. Turner, and L. Rosen. A multivariate analysis of female extramarital coitus. *Journal of Marriage and the Family* 37 (1975): 375–385.

Bergler, E. *Divorce Won't Help.* New York: Harper and Brothers, 1948, p. 11.

Bernard, J. The adjustments of married mates. In H. T. Christensen, ed., *Handbook of Marriage and the Family*. Chicago: Rand McNally, 1964, pp. 675–739.

Berne, E. *Games People Play*. New York: Grove Press, 1964.

Berscheid, E. Dependence in interpersonal attraction. Grant submitted to National Science Foundation, 1973.

Berscheid, E., and J. Fei. Romantic love and sexual jealousy. In G. Clanton and Lynn G. Smith, eds., *Jealousy*. Englewood Cliffs, N.J.: Prentice-Hall, 1977, pp. 101–109.

Berscheid, E., W. Stephan, and E. Walster. Sexual arousal and heterosexual perception. *Journal of Personality and Social Psychology* 20 (1971): 93–101.

Berscheid, E., E. Walster, and G. Bohrnstedt. The body image report. *Psychology Today* 7 (1973): 119–131.

Berscheid, E., E. Walster, and G. Bohrnstedt. Body image. *Psychology Today,* July 1972, pp. 57–66.

Blatt, C. S., and R. C. Blatt. An evolutionary theory of social interaction. Unpublished manuscript, 1970.

Blau, P. M. Social exchange. In D. L. Sills, ed., *International Encyclopedia of the Social Sciences*. Vol. VII. New York: Macmillan, 1968, pp. 452–457.

Blau, P. M. *Exchange and Power in Social Life*. New York: Wiley, 1964.

Blood, R. O., Jr. Romance and premarital intercourse—incompatibles? *Marriage and Family Living* 14 (1952): 105–108.

Blood, R. O., Jr., and D. M. Wolfe. *Husbands and Wives: The Dynamics of Married Living*. Glencoe, Ill.: The Free Press, 1960.

Blum, S. When can adultery be justified or forgiven? *McCall's,* May 1966.

Bohannan, P., ed. *Divorce and After*. Garden City, N.Y.: Doubleday/Anchor, 1971.

Breedlove, W., and J. Breedlove. *Swap Clubs*. Los Angeles: Sherbourne Press, 1964.

Brehm, J. W., M. Gatz, G. Goethals, J. McCrimmon, and L. Ward. Psychological arousal and interpersonal attraction. Mimeographed, 1970. (Available from authors.)

Brislin, R. W., and S. A. Lewis. Dating and physical attractiveness: a replication. *Psychological Reports* 22 (1968): 976.

Sir R. Burton and F. F. Arbuchnot. (Trans.) *The Kama Sutra*. New York: G. P. Putnam, p. 138.

Byrne, D. The influence of propinquity and opportunities for interaction on classroom relationships. *Human Relations* 14 (1961): 63–70.

Byrne, D., and J. A. Buehler. A note on the influence of propinquity upon acquaintanceships. *Journal of Abnormal and Social Psychology* 51 (1955): 147–148.

Byrne, D., and G. L. Clore. A reinforcement model of evaluative responses. *Personality: An International Journal* 1 (1970): 103–128.

Christensen, H. T., and C. F. Gregg. Changing sex norms in America and Scandinavia. *Journal of Marriage and the Family* 32 (1970) : 616–627.

Cimbalo, R. S., V. Faling, and P. Mousaw. The course of love: a cross-sectional design. *Psychological Reports* 38 (1976) : 1292–1294.

Clarke, A. C. An examination of the operation of residential propinquity as a factor in mate selection. *American Sociological Review* 17 (1952) : 17–22.

Clemens, L. G. Effect of stimulus female variation on sexual performance of the male deermouse, *peromyscus manifulatus. Proceedings of the American Psychological Association, 75th Annual Convention,* 1967, pp. 119–120.

Cohen, A., and I. Silverman. Repression-sensitization as a dimension of personality. In B. A. Maher, ed., *Progress in Experimental Personality Research.* Vol. 1. New York: Academic Press, 1964.

Davitz, J. R. *The.Language of Emotion.* New York: Academic Press, 1969.

DeLamater, J. D. Sociopsychological aspects of premarital conception. Reported in J. DeLamater and P. MacCorquodale, Premarital contraceptive use: a test for two models. Center for Demography and Ecology. Working Paper 76–24. Madison: University of Wisconsin, 1976.

Dement, W., and N. Kleitman. The relation of eye movements during sleep to dream activity, an objective method for the study of dreaming. *Journal of Experimental Psychology* 53 (1957) : 339–346.

de Rougemont, D. The crisis of the modern couple. In Ruth Nanda Anshen, ed., *The Family: Its Function and Destiny.* New York: Harper & Row, 1949, pp. 451–452.

Deutsch, M., and L. Solomon. Reactions to evaluations by others as influenced by self evaluations. *Sociometry* 22 (1959) : 93–112.

Douvan, E. Interpersonal relationships—some questions and observations. Presented at Raush Conference, 1974.

Dutton, D. G. Effect of feedback parameters on congruency versus positivity effects in reactions to personal evaluations. *Journal of Personality and Social Psychology* 24 (1972) : 366–371.

Elder, G. H., Jr. Appearance and education in marriage mobility. *American Sociological Review* 34 (1969) : 519–533.

Ellis, A. *The Civilized Couple's Guide to Extramarital Adventure.* New York: Wyden, 1972.

Ellis, A., and R. Harper. *Creative Marriage.* New York: Lyle Stuart, 1961.

Emerson, R. *Sociological Theories in Progress.* Boston: Houghton Mifflin, 1972.

Exline, R. Visual interaction: the glances of power and preference. In J. Cole, ed., *Nebraska Symposium on Motivation 1971.* Lincoln: University of Nebraska Press, 1972.

Fenichel, O. *The Psychoanalytic Theory of Neurosis.* London: Routledge & Kegan Paul, 1955.

Festinger, L. Architecture and group membership. *Journal of Social Issues* 1 (1951): 152–163.

Festinger, L. A theory of social comparison processes. *Human Relations* 7 (1954): 117–140.

Fisher, A. E. The effects of differential early treatment on the social and exploratory behavior of puppies. Ph.D. dissertation, Pennsylvania State University, University Park, 1955.

Fisher, W. A., and D. Byrne. Sex differences in response to erotica: love versus lust. *Journal of Personality and Social Psychology* 36 (1978): 117–125.

Fiske, D. W., and S. R. Maddi. The forms of varied experience, 1–10. In Donald W. Fiske and Salvatore R. Maddi, *Functions of Varied Experience*. Homewood, Ill.: The Dorsey Press, 1961.

Ford, C. S., and F. A. Beach. *Patterns of Sexual Behavior*. New York: Harper & Row, 1951.

Freud, S. *Collected Papers*. London: The Hogarth Press and the Institute for Psychoanalysis, 1933.

Freud, S. Certain neurotic mechanisms in jealousy, paranoia, and homosexuality. In *Collected Papers*. Vol. 2. London: Hogarth, 1922, pp. 235, 240, 323.

Freud, S. Creative writers and daydreaming. In J. Strachey, ed., *The Standard Edition of the Complete Psychological Works of Sigmund Freud*. Vol. 9. London: Hogarth, 1962a.

Fromm, E. *The Art of Loving*. New York: Harper & Row, 1956.

Galton, F. Measurement of character. *Fortnightly Review* 36 (1884): 179–185.

Gebhard, P. H. Fetishism and sadomasochism. In Martin S. Weinberg, ed., *Sex Research: Studies from the Kinsey Institute*. New York: Oxford University Press, 1976, pp. 156–166.

Géraldy, P. L'Amour. In William Geoffrey, ed., *The Compleat Lover*. New York: Harrison-Hilton Books, 1939, p. 7.

Goffman, E. On cooling the mark out: some aspects of adaptation to failure. *Psychiatry* 15 (1952): 451–463.

Goldberg, G. N., C. A. Kiesler, and B. E. Collins. Visual behavior and face-to-face distance during interaction. *Sociometry* 32 (1969): 43–53.

Goldstein, M. K. Increasing positive behaviors in married couples. In J. D. Krumholtz and C. E. Thoreson, eds., *Counseling Methods*. New York: Holt (in press).

Goode, W. J. *After Divorce*. Glencoe, Ill.: Free Press, 1956.

Gottschalk, H. *Skinsygens Problemer (Problems of Jealousy)*. Copenhagen: Fremand, 1936.

Grant, V. W. *Falling in Love*. New York: Springer, 1976.

Griffitt, W. Environmental effects on interpersonal affective behavior: ambient effective temperature and attraction. *Journal of Personality and Social Psychology* 15 (1970): 240–244.

Griffitt, W., J. May, and R. Veitch. Sexual stimulation and interpersonal behavior: heterosexual evaluative responses, visual behavior, and physical proximity. *Journal of Personality and Social Psychology* 30 (1974): 367–377.

Halverson, H. M. Infant sucking and tensional behavior. *Pedagogical Seminary and Journal of Genetic Psychology* 53 (1938): 365–430.

Halverson, H. M. Genital and sphincter behavior of the male infant. *Pedagogical Seminary and Journal of Genetic Psychology* 56 (1940): 95–136.

Hamilton, G. V. A study of sexual tendencies in monkeys and baboons. *Journal of Animal Behavior* 14 (1914): 301–302.

Harmsworth, H. C., and M. S. Minnis. Nonstatutory causes of divorce. The lawyer's point of view. *Marriage and Family Living* 17 (1955): 316–321.

Hartman, C. G. The mating of mammals. *Annual Meetings of the New York Academy of Science* 46 (1945): 39.

Herter, G. L. *How to Live with a Bitch*. Waseca, Minn.: Herter's, 1974.

Hill, C. T., Z. Rubin, and A. Peplau. Breakups before marriage: the end of 103 affairs. *Journal of Social Issues* 32 (1976): 147–167.

Hobart, C. W. The incidence of romanticism during courtship. *Social Forces* 36 (1958): 362–367.

Holmes, S. J., and C. E. Hatch. Personal appearance as related to scholastic records and marriage selection in college women. *Human Biology* 10 (1938): 65–76.

Homans, G. C. *Social Behavior: Its Elementary Forms*. Rev. ed. New York: Harcourt, Brace, Jovanovich, 1974.

Hoon, P. W., J. P. Wincze, and E. F. Hoon. A test of reciprocal inhibition. Are anxiety and sexual arousal in women mutually inhibitory? *Journal of Abnormal Psychology* 86 (1977): 65–74.

Hunt, M. *The Affair*. New York: World, 1969.

Hunt, M. *The World of the Formerly Married*. New York: McGraw-Hill, 1966.

Hupka, R. B. Societal and individual roles in the expression of jealousy. In H. Sigall (Chair), *Sexual Jealousy*. Symposium presented at the meeting of the American Psychological Association, San Francisco, August 1977, pp. 7–9.

"J." *The Sensuous Woman*. New York: Dell, 1969.

Katz, A. M., and R. Hill. Residential propinquity and marital selection: a review of theory, method, and fact. *Marriage and Family Living* 20 (1958): 327–335.

Kennedy, R. Pre-marital residential propinquity. *American Journal of Sociology* 48 (1943): 580–584.

Kerckhoff, A. C. The social context of interpersonal attraction. In T. L. Huston, ed., *Foundations of Interpersonal Attraction*. New York: Academic Press, 1974.

Kiesler, C. A., and G. N. Goldberg. Multidimensional approach to the experimental study of interpersonal attraction: effect of a blunder on the attractiveness of a competent other. *Psychological Reports* 22 (1968): 693–705.

Klinger, E. *Structure and Functions of Fantasy*. New York: Wiley, 1971.

Komarovsky, M. *The Unemployed Man and His Family*. New York: Octagon Books, 1971.

Krames, L., D. J. Costanzo, and W. J. Carr. Responses of rats to odors from novel versus original sex partners. *Proceedings of the American Psychological Association, 75th Annual Convention,* 1967, pp. 117–118.

Lagache, D. *La Jalousie Amoureuse*. Bibliotheque de Philosophie Contemporaine. Vols. I and II. Paris: Presses Universitaires de France, 1947.

Langfeldt, G. The erotic jealousy syndrome: a clinical study. *Acta Psychiatrica et Neurologica Scandinavica* 36, Supplementum 151 (1961): 7–68.

Law, O. T., and L. K. Gerbrandt. Sexual preference in female rats: I. Choices in tests with copulation. *Psychonomic Science* 8 (1967): 493–494.

Levinger, G. Marital dissatisfaction among divorce applicants. *American Journal of Orthopsychiatry* 36 (1966): 803–807.

Levinger, G. A social psychological perspective on marital dissolution. *The Journal of Social Issues* 32 (1976): 21–48.

Levinger, G., and J. Breedlove. Interpersonal attraction and agreement: a study of marriage partners. *Journal of Personality and Social Psychology* 3 (1966): 367–372.

Levy, R. I. *Tahitians*. Chicago: University of Chicago Press, 1973.

Libby, R. W., and R. N. Whitehurst, eds. *Renovating Marriage: Toward New Sexual Lifestyles*. Danville, Ca.: Consensus Publishers, 1973.

Lobsenz, N. M., and B. I. Murstein. Keeping score: it's fine for football games but it's disastrous for a marriage. *Woman's Day,* September 1976, pp. 146–154.

Locke, H. J. *Predicting Adjustment in Marriage: A Comparison of a Divorced and a Happily-Married Group*. New York: Holt, 1951, pp. 58–67.

Lott, A. J.. and B. E. Lott. Group cohesiveness, communication level and conformity. *Journal of Abnormal and Social Psychology* 62 (1961): 408–412.

Lott, A. J., and B. E. Lott. The role of reward in the formation of positive interpersonal attitudes. In T. L. Huston, ed., *Foundations of Interpersonal Attraction*. New York: Academic Press, 1974, pp. 171–189.

"M." *The Sensuous Man*. New York: Dell, 1972.

McCall, M. M. Courtship as social exchange: some historical comparisons. In Bernard Farber, ed., *Kinship and Family Organization*. New York: Wiley, 1966, pp. 190–200.

McCary, J. L. *Human Sexuality*. 2d ed. New York: Van Nostrand, 1973.

McDougall, W. *Introduction to Social Psychology*. London: Methuen and Company, 1908.

Mairet, A. *La Jalousie: Etude Psychophysiologique, Clinique et Medico-Legale.* Montpelier, 1908.

Maissonneuve, J., G. Palmade, and C. Fourment. Selective choices and propinquity. *Sociometry* 15 (1952): 135–140.

Malinowski, B. *Argonauts of the Western Pacific: An Account of Native Enterprise and Adventure in the Archipelagoes of Melanesian New Guinea.* New York: Dutton, 1922.

Maslow, A. H. *Motivation and Personality.* New York: Harper & Row, 1954.

Maslow, A. H., and N. L. Mintz. Effects of esthetic surroundings: I. Initial effects of three esthetic conditions upon perceiving "energy" and "well-being" in faces. *Journal of Psychology* 41 (1956): 247–254.

Masters, W. H., and V. E. Johnson. *The Pleasure Bond.* New York: Bantam Books, 1975.

Mead, M. Jealousy: primitive and civilized. In A. M. Krich, ed., *The Anatomy of Love.* New York: Dell, 1960.

Mettee, D. R., and E. Aronson. Affective reactions to appraisal from others. In Ted L. Huston, ed., *Foundations of Interpersonal Attraction.* New York: Academic Press, 1974, pp. 235–283.

Miller, G. S., Jr. The primate basis of human sexual behavior. *Quarterly Review of Biology* 6 (1931): 397–398, 406.

Mills, J. R. Social relationships and interpersonal attraction. Grant submitted to National Institute of Mental Health, 1976.

Morgan, M. *The Total Woman.* New York: Pocket Books, 1975.

Murray, H. A. *Explorations in Personality.* Oxford, England: Oxford University Press, 1938.

Murstein, B. I. Stimulus-value-role: a theory of marital choice. *Journal of Marriage and the Family* 32 (1970): 465–481.

Murstein, B. I. Physical attractiveness and marital choice. *Journal of Personality and Social Psychology* 22 (1972): 8–12.

Murstein, B. I. The relationship of mental health to marital choice and courtship progress. *Journal of Marriage and the Family* 29 (1967): 447–451.

Murstein, B. I., M. Goyette, and M. Cerreto. A theory of the effect of exchange orientation on marriage and friendship. Unpublished manuscript, 1974.

Neubeck, G. *Extramarital Relations.* Englewood Cliffs, N.J.: Prentice-Hall, 1969.

Patterson, G. R., and J. B. Reid. Reciprocity and coercion: two facets of social systems. In C. Neringer and J. L. Michael, eds., *Behavior Modification in Clinical Psychology.* New York: Appleton, 1970.

Peele, S., with A. Brodsky. *Love and Addiction.* New York: Taplinger, 1975.

Rappaport, A. F., and J. Harrell. A behavioral-exchange for marital counseling. *Family Coordinator* 21 (1972): 203–213.

Rosen, S., R. D. Johnson, M. J. Johnson, and A. Tesser. Interactive effects of news valence and attraction on communicator behavior. *Journal of Personality and Social Psychology* 28 (1973): 298–300.

Rosen, S., and A. Tesser. On reluctance to communicate undesirable information: the MUM effect. *Sociometry* 33 (1970): 253–263.

Rubin, Z. Measurement of romantic love. *Journal of Personality and Social Psychology* 16 (1970): 265–273.

Scanzoni, J. *Sexual Bargaining: Power Politics in the American Marriage*. Englewood Cliffs, N.J.: Prentice-Hall, 1972.

Schmidt, G. and V. Sigusch. Sex differences in response to psycho-sexual stimulation by films and slides. *Journal of Sex Research* 6 (1970): 268–283.

Schmidt, G., V. Sigusch, and S. Schafer. Responses to reading erotic stories: male-female differences. *Archives of Sexual Behavior* 2 (1973): 181–199.

Sears, R. E., E. Maccoby, and H. Levine. *Patterns of Child Rearing*. White Plains, New York: Paul Peterson, 1957.

Secord, P. F., and S. M. Jourard. The appraisal of body cathexis; body cathexis and the self. *Journal of Consulting Psychology* 17 (1953): 343–347.

Segal, M. W. Alphabet and attraction: an unobtrusive measure of the effect of propinquity in a field setting. *Journal of Personality and Social Psychology* 30 (1974): 654–657.

Shadle, A. R. Copulation in the porcupine. *Journal of Wildlife Management* 10 (1946): 160–161.

Shrauger, J. S. Response to evaluation as a function of initial self-perception. *Psychological Bulletin* 82 (1975): 581–596.

Shuttleworth, F. K. A biosocial and developmental theory of male and female sexuality. *Marriage and Family Living* 21 (1959): 163–170.

Silverman, I. Physical attractiveness and courtship. *Sexual Behavior,* September 1971, pp. 22–25.

Silverman, I. Self-esteem and differential responsiveness to success and failure. *Journal of Abnormal and Social Psychology* 69 (1964): 115–119.

Sokoloff, B. *Jealousy: A Psychiatric Study*. New York: Howell, Soskin, 1947.

Spuhler, J. N. Assortative mating with respect to physical characteristics. *Eugenics Quarterly* 15 (1968): 128–140.

Stendahl, M. (pseud.) *Love*. Trans. by Gilbert and Suzanne Sale. London: The Merlin Press, 1957.

Stephan, W., E. Berscheid, and E. Walster. Sexual arousal and heterosexual perception. *Journal of Personality and Social Psychology* 20 (1971): 93–101.

Storer, N. W. *The Social System of Science*. New York: Holt, Rinehart & Winston, 1966.

Strauss, A. Personality needs and marital choice. *Social Forces* 25 (March 1947): 332–335.

Sussman, M. B. Marriage contracts: social and legal consequences. Presented at the 1975 International Workshop on Changing Sex Roles in Family and Society, June 17, 1975.

Tesser, A., and M. Brodie. A note on the evaluation of a "computer date." *Psychonomic Science* 23 (1971): 300.

Traupmann, J. Equity and marriage: a test of equity theory with intimate relationships. Ph.D. dissertation, University of Wisconsin, 1977.

Traupmann, J. Equity and intimate relations. Ph.D. dissertation, University of Wisconsin, 1977.

Udry, J. R. *The Social Context of Marriage.* Philadelphia: J. B. Lippincott, 1971.

Utne, M. K. Equity and intimate relations: a test of the theory in marital interaction. Ph.D. dissertation, University of Wisconsin, 1977.

Valins, S. Cognitive effects of faulty heart-rate feedback. *Journal of Personality and Social Psychology* 4 (1966): 400–408.

Varni, C. A. An exploratory study of spouse-swapping. *Pacific Sociological Review* 15 (1972): 507–522.

Viorst, J. *Yes Married* (New York: Saturday Review Press, 1972).

Waller, W. *The Old Love and the New: Divorce and Readjustment.* Carbondale, Ill.: Southern Illinois University Press, 1958.

Waller, W. *The Family: A Dynamic Interpretation.* New York: Dryden, 1938.

Walster, E. Effect of self-esteem on liking for dates of various social desirabilities. *Journal of Experimental Social Psychology* 6 (1970): 248–253.

Walster, E., E. Aronson, and D. Abrahams. On increasing the persuasiveness of a low prestige communicator. *Journal of Experimental Social Psychology* 2 (1966): 325–342.

Walster, E., V. Aronson, D. Abrahams, and L. Rottman. The importance of physical attractiveness in dating behavior. *Journal of Personality and Social Psychology* 4 (1966): 508–516.

Walster, E., J. Traupmann, and G. W. Walster. Equity and extramarital sexuality. *Archives of Sexual Behavior* 7 (1978): 127–141.

Walster, E., G. W. Walster, and J. Traupmann. Equity and premarital sex. *Journal of Personality and Social Psychology* 37 (1978): 82–92.

Walster, E., G. W. Walster, J. Piliavin, and L. Schmidt. Playing hard-to-get: understanding an elusive phenomenon. *Journal of Personality and Social Psychology* 26 (1973): 113–121.

Weber, E. *How to Pick up Girls.* New York: Bantam, 1971.

Weiss, R. L., G. R. Birchler, and J. P. Vincent. Contractual models for negotiation training in marital dyads. *Journal of Marriage and the Family* 36 (1974): 321–331.

Weiss, R. L., H. Hops, and G. R. Patterson. A framework for conceptualizing marital conflict, a technology for altering it, some data for evaluating it. In L. A. Hamerlynck, L. C. Handy, and E. J. Mash, eds., *Behavior Change: Methodology, Concepts, and Practice.* Champaign, Ill.: Research Press, 1973.

Welch, J. J., and M. K. Goldstein. The differential effects of operant-interpersonal intervention. Manuscript submitted for publication, 1974.

Wells, L. E., and G. Marwell. *Self-esteem: Its Conceptualization and Measurement.* London: Sage, 1976.

Wickler, W. *The Sexual Code.* Garden City, N.J.: Doubleday, 1972.

Winch, Robert F. *Mate Selection: A Study of Complementary Needs.* New York: Harper & Row, 1958.

Wilson, E. O. *Sociobiology.* Cambridge, Mass.: The Belknap Press, 1975.

Wolfe, L. *Playing Around: Women and Extramarital Sex.* New York: Morrow, 1975.

Wylie, R. C. *The Self Concept.* Lincoln: University of Nebraska Press, 1961.

Zajonc, R. B. Attitudinal effects of mere exposure. *Journal of Personality and Social Psychology Monograph* 9 (1968): 1–20.

Zillman, D. Excitation transfer in communication-mediated aggressive behavior. *Journal of Experimental Social Psychology* 7 (1971): 419–434.

Zimbardo, P. *Shyness: What It Is, What to Do about It.* Reading, Mass.: Addison-Wesley, 1977.

Zuckerman, M. The sensation-seeking motive. In B. Maher, ed., *Progress in Experimental Personality Research.* Vol. 7. New York: Academic Press, 1974.

Index

Abnormal sexuality, defined, 101
Adultery, *see* Extramarital affairs
Affection
  and liking, 9
  withdrawal of, child's reaction to,
    6–7
Agape, 38, 39–40
Aggression and sex, 97–98
Allen, Woody, 23, 61
Altruistic love, 38, 39–40
Andelin, Helen B., 160
Androgenous beings, 5
Anger, and sexual arousal, 96–98
Anxiety, 120
  and sexual arousal, relationship
    between, 80–83
Aristotle, 46
Arousal, physiological, 8–9, 14, 58.
    See also Sexual arousal.
  and fantasies, 60–61
  measurement of, 63
Assessing a relationship, 153–158
Association, love by, 10–12
Attraction, 10
  by association, 10–12
  and fear, relationship between, 82–
    83
  and reinforcement, 10
  standing distance as index of, 13–
    14
"Attraction, Law of," 10

Attractiveness, physical, as desirable
    trait, 136–138, 149
  and socioeconomic status, relation-
    ship between, 139

Barclay, Andrew, 97
Beach, Frank, 75, 90
Beauty, love of, 38. *See also* Physical
    attractiveness.
Berscheid, Ellen, 141
Blau, Peter, 135
Blood, Robert O., 171
Body language, 14
  seduction through, 15
Boredom, sexual, 75, 112
Bowlby, John, 68–69
Breakups, 123–124, 168–169
  and extramarital sex, effect of,
    168–169
  initiation of, 124
Brown, Helen Gurley, 31
Bryson, Jeff, 89
Burgess, Ernest, 139
Byrne, Donn, 10, 13, 101
Byrne's "Law of Attraction," 10

Career women, 116–117
Carter, Jimmy, 26
Cartland, Barbara, 68
Child, Julia McWilliams, 26

201